The Paraeducator: The Other Grown-Up In The Classroom

Mary W. Hull

Mary Wenner Hull

The Paraeducator: The Other Grown-Up In The Classroom
Copyright © 2011 by Mary Wenner Hull

ISBN 978-0-9836427-0-1

Cover illustration by Rachel Marie Wenner (lastralor@gmail.com)
Photo by Susan F. Levine
Published by UpLearn, LLC (www.UpLearn.org)

UpLearn
P.O Box 46
Princeton, NJ 08642

Contact Mary W. Hull at marywhull@gmail.org
Or via her website at www.MaryWHull.org

Manufactured in the United States of America

Dedication

To my colleagues, "Pat", "Tiffany", "Ellen", "Babs", "Brenda" and "Kelsey".

Table of Contents

List of Tables

Preface

This book is a collaborative effort for which I owe many people thanks, but most especially the paraeducators who shared with me their stories of their personal and professional lives. I thank other colleagues at "Water Wheel" school for their help.

I am grateful for the opportunity to do research at the Graduate School of Education at Rutgers. Thanks to Drs. Jim Giarelli, Beth Rubin and Dr. David L. Keiser (cooperating from Montclair University). I appreciate their twin gifts of time and suggestions. I was also fortunate in the chairperson of my dissertation committee, Dr. Benjamin Justice. He taught me to see the panoply of policies, changes and school life through a historian's eyes. While the initial work for this book was done under the auspices of Rutgers, I continued interpretation and writing a year beyond their oversight. Any errors or omissions are entirely my own.

I also must include a grateful acknowledgement of Dr. Lynn Lederer, classmate at Rutgers, founder of our writers' group and friend.

Thanks to my family: my husband Art Hull for his deep reservoir of good nature, my daughter Rachel Wenner who took time from her own writing to edit mine, my son Daniel Wenner (Rutgers,'01) as my 'sponsor' to Rutgers, to the members of the Bernard clan and Hull family for their support, and to my sister Ellen Shrager, fellow educator and author, for her practical advice.

One participant told me: "I hope something good comes out of this." I, too, hope this book will contribute to an increased understanding of how paraeducators work with teachers and students.

Introduction

I am moving quickly down the A wing hall during second period, when I see Ellen[1], a paraeducator, and two students. Ellen sits at a low table with Mandy and Stefan, fourth graders who are classified as special education students. She shows them a hand-printed index card with the word "transpiration" and a drawing on it. As to be expected with children who are over a year below grade level in reading, Ellen is reading the term and its definitions to them. She sees me and makes eye contact, and nods at the children. She is teaching the terms for tomorrow's science test.

Ellen is sitting in the hallway as the inadvertent result of a special education reform. The employment of paraeducators like Ellen has increased dramatically in recent years. The United States Department of Education estimated that the members of this occupation grew in numbers by 123% from approximately 306,000 in the school year 1985-1986 to 685,000 in 2003-04. During the same period, the school-aged population only grew 23%.[2] The use of paraeducators is the most frequently used special education intervention.[3] Using paraeducators to assist children classified as eligible for special education and related services is really an

---

[1] All place names and names of participants have been changed to pseudonyms.

[2] (U.S. Dept. of Education, 2006).

[3] SPeNSE, 2000.

unintended consequence of the reform of inclusion. Under the term paraprofessional, instructional assistant or paraeducator, school administrators employed adults to meet federal legislation to include children classified as eligible for special education in as many general education classes as possible, under a provision in the law called "the least restrictive environment".[4]

Yet, their role and impact is not thoroughly studied: only 7 studies appeared between 1999 and 2007.[5] In contrast, I found six studies during the same time period for a less frequently used intervention: a surround sound system for use with hard of hearing, deaf or students with forms of central auditory processing disorder. In a school with over 800 students during the year of this study, only 1 child used the sound system while instructional assistants supported 72 children. The ratio of research studies to number of children involved suggested to me a need for investigation and consideration of the profession.

If the studies which directly examine the nature of the paraeducator's relationship with teachers and students are few in number, the research that asks the opinions of the paraeducator are fewer still.[6] Ellen's presence is as much serendipitous as it is under-examined. She has little opportunity to contribute to public discourse about her work. Due to low status within the school hierarchy, her voice has been muted in the public conversation. Giving a paraeducator like Ellen a vehicle to add to the public discourse is critical to understanding the value and complexity of their contribution to education. I wanted their voices and actions to shine through the written words and offer their unique perspective.

---

[4] PL94-142
[5] Nevin, et al., 2008.
[6] Bernal and Aragon 2004; Chopra et al 2004; Downing et al. 2000, French 2004;Milner, 1998.

Chapter One
Questions About The Occupation Of Paraeducator

My own involvement with paraeducators in general education classes began in the spring of 1997, when I received an administrative directive from my supervisor to maximize the amount of time each special education child spends in general education classes. The children needed support if they were going to be performing above their functional academic level, I reasoned, and a paraeducator could give the adapted instruction devised by teachers. Given the enormity of the switch, the lack of time to train teachers and the large class sizes in general education, I felt that assigning another adult to the classroom was a good intervention. My decision was spontaneous, in the moment, as a quick response to an immediate problem that was landing in my lap without a planned increase in resources or a plan for implementation. If I balanced the extra burden of individualizing instruction for a child with a disability with extra help, I thought the teachers would welcome the child. I thought my decision was made on my own, in isolation, with input from only a few other key staff. I routinely began to include the use of paraeducators in my plans for classified children in general education classes.

I was not alone. By the next year, most of the plans I received from other schools contained the same suggestion. I was part of a larger trend. Other people in my position recognized the paraeducator as a resource.

During the same period, I began my doctoral courses and a search for a worthy research topic. My thoughts turned to the paraeducators, whose work lives seemed to overflow with contradictions. They were outsiders, trying to become insiders, charged with assisting children to navigate the border from special education into general education. Many were mothers and members of the community, that is, laypeople, who were interacting with professional school people. Their use, first seen as an expedient and perhaps temporary support, was becoming institutionalized but controversial.

For despite the widespread employment of paraeducators in classrooms, many researchers have framed the paraeducators' teaching role in the classroom as a problem fraught with confused role boundaries.[7] One group of researchers concluded from a review of twenty-six articles on paraeducators that 58% of the material focused on the role of paraeducators and 42% discussed their training.[8] The role of the paraeducator and their training are two areas of the occupation that are reiterated in the literature, suggesting that these key aspects are problematic. By focusing upon the individual paraeducator, researchers imply that the failure of the reform to enfold a wider range of students into the classroom is either in the use of paraeducators as an intervention or the fault of the individual paraeducator.

From this stance, these researchers are engaged in a limited and limiting argument. If researchers discuss role using the individual paraeducator as the unit of analysis, then the individual paraeducator's behavior becomes the problem. Some researchers place the locus of control and agency in the hands of the individual paraeducator. I observed limited agency or control in the hands of these women and certainly nothing to suggest that they could

---

[7] Giangreco, 2003; Levine, 1999, Riggs, 2001, York-Barr, 2003) and a lack of training (Chopra et al, 2004; Downing, 2000; French, 2004; Giangreco, 1999, Hughes, 1993; Milner, 1998.
[8] Giangreco, et al, 2001.

single handedly ensure the success or failure of a child in an elementary classroom.

A paraeducator is part of an organization. A paraeducator does not perform her work in isolation.[9] A paraeducator performs complex labor in which meanings are shaped by the capacity of the teacher and students in the classes in which she works, the context in which the work takes place, their own innate capacities and their social and cultural experiences. She can influence only one factor, training, but has no control over either her past experiences, her innate capacities or the socio-cultural context of her work.

Some researchers debate just what training should include.[10] Training becomes problematic because training presumes an understanding of what their job entails. What are they doing and how are they supposed to do it?

Underneath the concrete activities of daily life in a classroom are shared assumptions and negotiations about how to apply those common ideas.[11] Through this shared practice, people create identity and learn. [12] From observation, I noticed that the paraeducators spent time in many more informal discussions than I did. I surmised that they needed to spend more time talking informally to co-workers because they have less formal delineation of role within the school. If paraeducators meet work demands and construct the meaning of their work socially through face-to-face interaction, then I reasoned that research into how they engage socially is a fruitful method of inquiry into their relationships with teachers and children.

---

[9] French, 2004; Riggs, 2001.
[10] Giangreco, 2003; Carroll, 2001
[11] Wenger, 1999, p.264.
[12] Wenger, 1999.

Chapter 1 Questions About The Occupation Of Paraeducator

By talking to Ellen and a group of paraeducators[13] like Ellen, I found valuable insider knowledge about their role in the classroom. From that information, I offer a textured description and analysis of their experiences to make visible the social assumptions underlying their work. Their individual accomplishments are determined in large part by the success or failure of their working relationships. To fully understand how they make, build and maintain the relationships that constitute their work, I incorporated their words and a description of their actions into the discussion and explored situational aspects of their occupation.

Following the practice of post-modern feminist writers, I include the voice of stakeholders in this discussion so that people hear from the ordinary women who perform this collective work. This story, while focusing on six individuals, is not about heroes or heroines, but about individuals who cooperate and work in concert, knowing that they are part of a group or at least a partnering enterprise. The sense of partnering within this occupation and the necessity to subordinate their will to the needs of others comes through in their narratives. As Gloria Steinem enjoins: "We are each other's heroes."[14]

While some roles in society, such as doctor and police officer, are no longer seen as almost exclusively male, the paraeducator is,

---

[13] For the sake of clarity, I will use the term "paraeducator" throughout this book, except when directly quoting an author or a participant who use other terms. Both paraeducator and paraprofessional are terms used interchangeably in research literature. On Sept. 21, 2011, the National Resource Center for Paraprofessionals changed its name to the National Resource Center for Paraeducators. In school districts, they are also called teaching aides, teaching assistants or instructional assistants depending upon local usage as other researchers such as Carrol, 2004 have noted.

[14] Steinem, in conversation after lecture remarks at the Yale Club, Feb. 2010.

especially at the elementary school level, almost always female. [15] Not one study explored or acknowledged the genderized nature of the occupation or the political freight that an occupation populated by women brings.

As a genderized role performed in a genderized space, the women who perform this role have made some assumptions and negotiations with their identity. Each participating paraeducator defined her identity and role within the classroom. In order to understand how she fulfills the role, I asked about her personal story that led her to this occupation, to learn the job and her perceptions of the responsibilities of the role. By asking how she establishes mutual understanding of expectations and solves problems, I probed her with questions about how she perceives her relationship to the teachers and students. Clandinin and Connelly describe narrative inquiry as, "...a way of understanding experience... as collaboration between researcher and participants..."[16]

What does Ellen do with the children? How does she know what to do? Is she a teacher? Public discourse has centered on answering these questions by investigating her work in the same way that a teacher's work is examined. Yet, she is not a teacher. That elusive sense of her being something other than a teacher is hard to define, unless the context of her work is examined.

---

[15] Since all the participants in this study are female, I use the pronouns "she" and "her" throughout this book.

[16] Morgan-Fleming, Riegle and Fryer, *Narrative Inquiry,* 81.

Chapter Two
Nestling The Questions Into Context

Paraeducators work in the area of schooling called "Special Education." Special education is the term for schooling that is beyond the usual and devised for a targeted group of children who do not learn as well as or under the same conditions as their peers. In the current special education system, school personnel judge that a child either has a deficit that puts him or her beyond normal expectations or has not responded to academic interventions with the expected rate of learning acquisition.

For the child who is classified as eligible for special education, general education has failed in some way. The burden of learning is no longer on him or her. The responsibility is no longer on his or her classroom teachers either, since they are not "special" educators. Responsibility moves to special education teachers and to auxiliary personnel, including the paraeducators.

I overheard one father inform his son, who was happy to be in a small class for reading instruction: "It is not an honor." That is true. These students occupy a place in the school that does not garner praise and can easily be marginalized, as can the adults in the school who work with them. Paraeducators assigned to marginalized students are themselves easily marginalized by association and because they possess little formal power within the school hierarchy[17]. Indeed, they can become the scapegoat for

---

[17] In contrast, in order to be an advocate for these easily marginalized children, I am given both responsibility and agency by law and practice.

failure of either the student, the teacher, or of the reform of inclusion that is codified in the law of the land.

While placing a second adult in a classroom is a simple concept, the practice has emerged from a complex history of laws, court decisions and policies that constitute the concept of special education. The paraeducators' entry to classroom can be best understood by viewing the larger historical context in which their profession is embedded.

Federal statutes.

Over the course of the history of the American republic, people have held competing views of what public schools are supposed to accomplish and this debate continues. David Labaree argues "that at the heart of the U.S. educational system is a fundamental ambivalence about whether education should be considered primarily a public good (one that is inclusive, providing shared societal benefits) or a private good (one that is exclusive, providing selective individual benefits)."[18] From a citizen's perspective, schools maintain the republic through training future citizens in democratic beliefs. From an employer's and/or taxpayer's perspective, schools train students for the workforce for social efficiency. From the consumer's point of view, the school provides a means to compete for social positions providing a promise for potential social mobility.[19] The special education laws rests primarily on an argument for democratic equality with equal access to the public schools, codified in the law PL94-142.

The provisions of PL94-142 did not specify where this guaranteed right to a free, appropriate education at public expense was to take place. Access to the public school building was not

---

[18] Labaree, 1997, p.5.
[19] Labaree, 1997.

access to the general education classroom. In some instances, children transferred from private special education schools to "schools within schools."[20] Children could become isolated within a public school.

In many cases, the children in the special education classes only saw their general education peers during lunch, recess and physical education classes.[21] Many parents wanted their children in regular classrooms with their peers. Their desire could and did clash with the nature of mass schooling. Teachers in most public school classrooms teach through group instruction, which does not always meet the instructional needs of children with learning difficulties. Experts describe individualized approaches to teaching children with disabilities, more suited for small groups or private tutorials.[22] PL94-142 straddles two trends in thinking about how children learn and where they should learn that can be contradictory: the trend to individualize instruction and a desire to teach all students in general education classes. [23]

With the passing of The Individuals with Disabilities Education Act (IDEA) of 1997, the federal government encouraged schools to instruct students classified as eligible for special education in general education classrooms. Until IDEA of 1997, there was no mention of paraeducators in the law. They earned a few scant lines when they were authorized by the federal government to "assist in the provision of special education and related services to children with disabilities (IDEA 97, section 300)."[24] Paraeducators in the public schools shifted from performing primarily clerical and disciplinary duties to fulfilling roles as academic instructors of

---

[20] Labaree, 1997.
[21] Water Wheel School, 2004
[22]Shaywitz, 2003.
[23] Blair and Sailor, 2005.
[24] US Government law

special needs children. [25] Local school districts decided upon the requirements for the position and in some, these requirements did not include a high school diploma. The 2001 federal law, known as No Child Left Behind, outlined training requirements for paraeducators that included a minimum of a high school diploma and some post high school training.

The revision of IDEA in 2004 (IDEIA, The Individuals with Disabilities Education Improvement Act), offered a job description of paraeducator services. In the New Jersey statute which incorporated and interpreted the federal statute, the creators of the law gave the paraeducator a job description "including, but not limited to" [26] getting the student to participate, reinforcing goals, organizing activities and materials and using teacher created reinforcement activities. The law also stipulates that the paraeducator will be given time in the workday for consultation with the teacher or teachers in charge of the students they work with on a regular basis (State of New Jersey, 2006).[27] With the exception of officially scheduled time for collaboration, the law codified and mirrored what I had observed taking place in practice in my district.

Landmark court cases in special education

Educational historians attribute the development of special education to several roots. Lawrence Cremin observed, "The revolution inherent in the idea that everyone ought to be educated had created both the problem and the opportunity of the Progressives.[28] Bowles and Gintis, however, see the reform as "the

---

[25] French, 2004;Bernal, 2004.
[26] IDEIA (p.67)"
[27] Sate of New Jersey, 2006
[28] Cremin, 1961, p.ix.

Chapter 2:   Nestling the Questions Into Context

displacement of social problems into the school systems."[29] David Tyack notes "schooling was a ritual process that acquired political significance because people believed in it." [30] Whatever the political sources, schooling also gained legal significance. Through court decisions such as the Brown v. The Board of Education of Topeka[31], federal judges defined education as a civil right. [32]

Some parents of handicapped children and their advocates learned strategies from the civil rights movement and appealed to the federal government for laws and court rulings to give their children a public education. This body of law created far reaching changes that affected every school because "the law made refusal to educate illegal and participation in schooling mandatory" [33]

Through advocates, some parents and guardians argued that this civil right, guaranteed by law without a bar by race, should be a civil right without a bar by handicap. Some parents brought suit against school districts on the basis of anti-discrimination laws in cases such as the 1971 case of Pennsylvania Association for Retarded Children (PARC) v. Commonwealth of Pennsylvania.[34] Plaintiffs in this case challenged a state ruling that unless a child had attained a mental age of five by first grade entry, he or she could be denied school services by their district. Basic tenets of the reform under the PL94-142 of 1975 were delineated in this ruling: the state must provide a free, appropriate, public education for children with mental retardation up to the age of 21.[35] In 1972, the case of Mills v. Board of Education (of the District of Columbia)

---

[29] Bowles and Gintis, p.53.
[30] Tyack, 1995, p. 157.
[31] Brown vs. The board of Education of Topeka, 1954.
[32] Borden, 2004.
[33]Sarason, 1996.
[34] PARC, 1971
[35] Ibid, PARC

18

settled a suit brought on the behalf of children who were denied public school enrollment based only upon their disability.[36] The court interpreted the equal protection clause of the 14th amendment to ensure children full due process and equal access to a meaningful education.

These equal protection rights were also upheld by the federal courts in over thirty rulings between 1971 and 1973, for children who are designated as eligible for special education.[37] Through their representatives, some parents of children with special needs lobbied a receptive Congress to pass legislation to give handicapped children the same right to education as their non-handicapped peers. Through the power of statute and case law, children who had been previously barred from classrooms would now have a public education.

A solution to a contradiction

There was a precedent and a model of non-professionals already in place in the schools who could be assigned to help a child learn in the general education classes. With the "baby boom" of the post World War II era and resultant teacher shortages, people with less training, almost universally female, were hired to work in the schools helping with clerical work and supervision of children during non-instructional time. The employment of these workers, paraeducators, became the solution to an institution's inherent contradiction, like other instances of school reform. [38]

The contradiction in this case is that children with individual needs that had precluded them from mass education would now access that form of education through individualized adaptation.

---

[36] Mills decision
[37] Franklin, 1994.
[38] Ibid, Franklin.

Chapter 2: Nestling the Questions Into Context

Teachers would not need to stop teaching children in groups nor change how they taught children. Under a teacher's direction, the other adult in the classroom changes a mass education system, a "one size fits almost all" approach to schooling, to a specific measure that would support the child in ways unique to that child. This evolution in the underlying structure of schooling, the "grammar" of schooling. [39] Because this is a fundamental change in the basic structure of schools, it creates an inherent tension through grafting a new idea onto an old institution.[40]

Thus, the growing use of paraeducators can be seen as an inadvertent reform influenced by the historical trend of increased inclusion in public schools.[41] The public judges reforms for success or failure of a reform based upon information created by two groups. The first group includes experts, such as researchers and policy makers, and the second group includes practitioners, such as teachers and school officials.

Cuban argues that the criteria these two groups use are often not made explicit, but should be.[42] According to his analysis, experts, whom Cuban calls the policymaking elite, look at three criteria. First, they consider the effectiveness of the reform by asking if the reform's intended goals have been met. Secondly, they consider the popularity of the reform as measured by the widespread use of the reform and support from the public. Thirdly, experts judge a reform by how closely the reform stays true to the original design when it is in practice.

Practitioners, on the other hand, look for adaptability and longevity in a reform. They value flexibility and sustained use. The

---

[39]Tyack, 1995.
[40] Cuban, 1993
[41] Tyack, 1995
[42] Cuban, 1998

paraeducators' value to practitioners may explain the growing use of paraeducators in the schools, despite the experts' concerns that paraeducators may prevent the true inclusion of handicapped students into the general education classroom in the original spirit of the federal laws.[43]

Public Discussion

In a study discussing paraeducators' perceptions of how they help connect the school to the community, Chopra and her research associates conceptualized the role of paraeducator as one of connector, as the hub of many relationships, in which the paraeducator connects the student to the teacher, the student to the curriculum, the parent and the teacher, and the student with other students.[44] Forty-nine paraeducators answered questions about their relationships with their school and their community through focus groups. The participants were self-selected from among people attending a paraeducators' conference and came from a variety of school settings.

Paraeducators expressed their relationship to the students in a variety of similes invoking family members. They compared themselves to an older sister or a grandmother, while the teacher was the parent. Some of the paraeducators believed that they were more available to students, both in school and in their communities, than the teachers because they were more visible in both settings. Some felt that the students were more comfortable with them because they served to support them, while the teacher was the disciplinarian. Paraeducators also reported that they played an important role in connecting teachers and students, most especially when the paraeducator and the student shared the same

---

[43] Giangreco, 2004
[44] Chopra et al., 2004

primary language. Part of the study focused on the paraeducators' instructional role, expressed as a role in connecting students to the curriculum. Many noted that they could re-teach group lessons on a one-to-one basis.

These observations prompted the researchers to ask how they knew how to adapt the curriculum, and the paraeducators replied that they had learned through observation of teachers. The teachers were seen as their models, and one participant said: "A lot has come from observing the teachers and working side by side with them".[45] Two researchers noted that the paraeducators' they surveyed put a strong focus on relationships:

> "Perhaps the most striking aspect of the research was the paraeducators' acknowledgment of the complex and intense relationships that developed between various members of the school community. Survey respondents indicated that their relationships with staff (as evidenced by participation in staff meetings and demonstrations of respect by colleagues) were important to them."[46]

The suggested sense of identity, role and participation in a community of practice is consistent with how I envision the conceptual framework for examining their work.

Conceptual Framework

The researchers describe an occupation open to many interpretations, and thus, with a strong potential for confusion. To clarify my position within this discussion, I want to delineate several key terms.

---

[45] Chopra et al, 2004, p.75.
[46] Riggs and Mueller, 2001, p.7.

Identity

My work builds on previous research into "discourse of identity" in education.[47] Discourse of identity research pulls from a variety of methodologies developed by researchers in a wide swath of intellectual territory that includes sociology, psychology, cultural theory and education.[48] Integrating this area gives a rationale for analysis of the information the participants shared.

Psychological and social development researchers locate identity at the frontier between the individual's ego and his or her social and cultural surroundings. Identity is then the outcome of the pull between personal self and social persona.[49] In this sense, identity is defined as a two-fold process in which role, identified as social needs and interests, plays a large part.

In the tradition of sociology and psychology, a person invents and constructs his or her own identity.[50] Other theorists believe that the individual and the world have a reciprocal relationship in which they constantly work on building each other. During this mutual construction, there is a potential for struggle between the individual and the surrounding world over contradictions and differences in understandings.

As a way to explain this potential conflict, a person can tell him or herself a story that is different from other people's versions of the world.[51] By creating a personal story, he or she gains a sense of his or her own action through choices, that is, agency.[52] Through narrative discourse, a person continuously creates an ongoing

---

[47] Juzwik, 2006; Sfard and Prusak, 2005.
[48] Juzwik, 2006.
[49] Reich, 2000.
[50] Erikson, 1968;Marshall, 1994.
[51] Fitch, 2003.
[52] Giroux, 1997

formation of identity.[53] According to these two authors, people shape their identity through creating two types of narratives: narrative of "actual identities" and narrative of "designated identities".[54] People create actual identities from stories about how things are now and their designated identities arise from stories about how things are expected to be, either now or in the future. In the view of Sfard and Prusak, identity is not an unchanging core, but a process built through narrative because they are "discursive counterparts of one's lived experiences".[55] The stories a paraeducator tells herself about herself, the process of the invention of those stories, combined with her physical/emotional/mental capacity becomes her identity.

Psychologist Warren Reich attests that identity is complex and multifaceted. He states that most personality and social development theorists agree that identity resides at the interface between an individual ego and the surrounding social and cultural milieu and represents a resolution of the dialectic between the needs and interests of self-identification and of social identification.[56] He asserts that core identity exists. If a person has some characteristics that they identify with that are immutable, that would constitute a core identity.[57] Although Reich does not explicitly link this concept to role, he implies that some roles are more compelling than others and are more resistant to transformation or mutability. If a role lessens in importance, or even ceases, the person's memory of that role becomes part of their identity. "Bodies as agents in social practice are involved in the

---

[53] Sfard and Prusak, 2005
[54] Ibid
[55] Ibid, p.18.
[56] Brewer, 1991; Erickson, 1968;McCall and Simmons, 1978 as cited in Reich, 1991.
[57] Reich, 1991

very construction of the social world, the bringing-into-being of social reality. The social world is never simply reproduced. It is always reconstituted by practice...Any situation admits of a range of possible responses".[58] I define identity more closely with the socio-cultural theorists who believe that some roles are more central than others to some people and that people are in a continuous state of "becoming" through the stories they tell themselves to give meaning to the events in their lives.

Theorists in this tradition emphasize the importance of language in creating identity. Researcher Frank Fitch asked: "if identity is ideologically constructed within discourse, in what sense is agency of resistance possible?" Although he was considering the identity of special education students, his question is relevant for paraeducators as well. He references Foucault, who "suggested that power produces reality".[59] Fitch concluded that students' identities were subject to circumstances.[60] So, too are paraeducators' identities.

Figured worlds.

Circumstances, as discussed by Fitch, are a part of context.[61] Context, such as the school and the individual classrooms within the school can make up what Dorothy Holland describes as a figured world. A figured world is a "socially and culturally constructed realm of interpretation in which particular characters and actors are recognized, significance is assigned to certain acts, and particular outcomes are valued over others."[62] A figured world is an imagined world "in which interpretations of human

---

[58] Connell, R.W. p.51
[59] Foucault
[60] Fitch, 2003
[61] Ibid.
[62] Holland et al, 1998, p. 52

actions are negotiated."[63] It is real to the participants, and it is a site where the participants negotiate interpretations of what is said and done and ascribe meaning to what is said and done. This world draws upon and is nestled in the context of meanings and interpretations that exist in a larger world. Holland suggests that people behave in a way that is only one of many possible ways of behaving available to them, but their range of choices is circumscribed by their status and power within the hierarchy.[64]

Thus, the paraeducators' identity is bound up with their participation in a world that has been conceptually agreed upon by them and the other participants. A figured world can be a place organized around common goals, such as a work site or a school. This figured world has much in common with Wenger's theory of how learning takes place within a community of practice.[65]

Community of practice

Looking at a school and the classrooms within a school as communities of practice offers a lens through which that the paraeducator's role does not stand alone, but is part of a bigger context. A group of people engaged with each other in actions they identify as their shared goal and using a shared set of behavior and resources they develop over time, comprise a community of practice.[66] People create ideas that influence what they do, and in turn, what they do influences their sense of identity.[67] Wenger suggests that this is a reciprocal process that creates social space as well as

---

[63] Ibid, p. 271
[64] Holland et al, 1998
[65] Wenger, 1999.
[66] Ibid.
[67] Holland, 1998;Wenger, 1999.

identity. He states that people learn through engagement in a community of practice.[68]

Although an informal social construct, Wenger says that there are fourteen observable characteristics to a community of practice. Among them are: sustained mutual relationships, shared ways of doing things engaged as a group, quick movement of information and learning new things, "absence of introductory preambles, as if conversations and interactions were merely the continuation of an ongoing process ", overlap in participants descriptions of who belongs, mutually defined identities, and a local lore such as inside jokes, jargon and a shared discourse.[69] Wenger notes "the ability to assess the appropriateness of actions and products" which would grow out of a shared sensibility and mutual definitions.[70] Additionally, he notes the ability to quickly set up a problem to be discussed, knowing what others can contribute to an enterprise, specific tools and artifacts, as well as shared styles and shared discourse that reflects a certain perspective on the world.

Wenger also states that the shared set of resources, what he calls "repertoire," has been built through a shared history and it "remains inherently ambiguous ".[71] It is the interplay of this ambiguity and history that results in a continuous negotiation of meaning and identity through actions and discussions within the community of practice and the individual's interpretation of these events. These characteristics are useful for the purposes of this book because participant and observer alike can describe and report instances that give evidence for both the existence of a community of practice and the place of people within that community. The concept also lends itself to a feminist lens by regarding

---

[68] Wenger, 1999.
[69] Wenger, 1999, p.125.
[70] Ibid.
[71] Ibid, p. 83.

the work as a cooperative venture rather than a heroic labor. I use these characteristics as part of the conceptual framework.

Role

Two theorists suggested that the idea of "role" forms a useful analytical bridge between the individual and the social levels of their culture.[72] The way we join society is through taking a role and when we try to do what is expected of us by others we are engaged in a role. That definition allows for a sense of social pressure and some room for variety in response to those expectations and to particular contexts, beyond the inherent reciprocity in the word "relationships". The importance of role in the literature on paraeducators reflects the importance of place within the hierarchy of schools.

A central preoccupation of the literature has been a search for that place. What is the paraeducator's role? He or she is not a student, like the learners in the class. Nor is he or she a teacher. The teacher is trained through the process of certification. The paraeducator gains authority and expertise through moving from the position of an outsider to that of a knowledgeable insider.

This movement in a social system mirrors the predicted behaviors of people in a community of practice.[73] Wenger asserts that there "is a profound connection between identity and practice ".[74] Both practice and identity hinge upon negotiated experience, membership, boundaries, a history of learning and connection to larger meanings.[75]

---

[72] Stryker and Statham, 1985
[73] Wenger, 1999;Holland, et al, 10998
[74] Wenger, 1999, p. 149.
[75] Ibid.

The Paraeducator: The Other Grown-Up In The Classroom

The interplay of elements in the conceptual framework

The paraeducators' role influences the development of their identity and their identity influences how they learn, perform and perceive the role. Some theorists, grouped as social constructivists, assert that learning is done in a social context.[76] This view is particularly appropriate for a discussion of paraeducators because they gain their expertise through on the job training in the classroom with teachers and students.

According to Lave and Wenger, people move from performing peripheral tasks in the environment to full participation in the central tasks of the work site. Knowledge is located in the relations between the expert practitioners and the novice.[77] This apprenticeship is more than learning by participation. They state, "For newcomers the purpose is not to learn from talk as a substitute for legitimate peripheral participation, it is to learn to talk as a key to legitimate peripheral participation."[78] Or, as another researcher phrases it: "Learning does not belong to individual persons, but to the various conversations of which they are a part."[79] In that spirit, conversations form the heart of this book.

[76] Gredler and Green, 2002
[77] Lave and Wenger, 1991
[78] Ibid, p. 108-109
[79] McDermott in Murphy, 1999, p.17

Chapter Three
A Way Of Looking For Answers

Paraeducators conversed with me based upon research questions that we investigated in the setting in which the work occurs, using exploratory approaches. To understand the actions I observed, I asked questions of those performing them. Actions cannot be understood without knowing the meaning that the participants ascribe to them. "Context, setting, and the participants' frames of reference" is the area of this qualitative research.[80] Constructs such as identity, role and relationship are unseen in the literal and concrete world but are signaled by people's thoughts, expressed through words.

Research Method

In this book, I used interviews to learn how the paraeducators perceive the relationships they have with the teachers and students with whom they work, and observations of each participant to portray the context of their work. I wrote notes to myself about incidents I witnessed throughout the book, from January through June, to capture informal discussions and events.

I conducted a series of three 40-minute interviews with each participant over the course of those six months. I used Kvale's views of an interview: "a semi-structured life world interview is defined as an interview whose purpose is to obtain descriptions of

---

[80] Marshall and Rossman, 1999, p.58

the life world of the interviewee with respect to interpreting the meaning of described phenomena".[81]

I observed one participant for a full day during each month and observed each of the other five participants for one period during that same month. I rotated the observations and the interviews so that I worked with each participant every month on a formal basis at least one time. There were opportunities for unscheduled, informal discussions with the six participants as the book progressed and my relationship with them developed. Additional information arose through channels unforeseen, such as a letter and emails from the participants.

Site

The major lure of this site was the match in class and education of the paraeducators with the teachers. In addition, I was fortunate in several other criteria: the district is in the top tier of districts statewide, according to the rankings created by the New Jersey State Department of Education. It is a well-resourced, suburban district, with a history of nimble adaptation to change and a commitment to inclusion.

I used five criteria for the school: a reputation for academic excellence, a substantial number of children classified as eligible for special education in general education class, a research-worthy number of paraeducators serving those children, accessibility and support for the research from the school administration.

Of the 868 children who attended fourth and fifth grade at the Water Wheel School during the 2007-2008 school year, 103 of the children who attended the school had identified disabilities. Children with disabilities are concentrated at Water Wheel School

---

[81] Kvale, 1996, p. 5-6

because Water Wheel contains many specialized programs, such as a class for pre-school handicapped, two classes for children with autism for grades one through five and a class for children with multiple disabilities in grades four through five. Children with handicaps can be seen in the halls, and importantly for my enquiry, in the general education classrooms. Of the 103 children who are eligible for special education, 76 attend general education classrooms. Of those 76, 72 are supported at some point in the day by a paraeducator.

In addition, the pool of teachers who teach classified children in general education classes is correspondingly large. Thirty–two of the thirty-five general education teachers work with paraeducators. The site was like the unacknowledged character in a work of fiction, with a character unique, specific and crucial to the unfolding of the novel.

Participants

The potential participants were invited to join this book based upon their employment status at the Water Wheel School as paraeducators who support children classified as eligible for special education in general education classrooms. Furthermore, to be included, these paraeducators had to be scheduled to give students this support for at least two forty-minute school periods daily in general education programs. Fifteen paraeducators met these criteria during the 2007-2008 school year.

Due to my membership on the Child Study Team at the Water Wheel School and the potential for conflict of interest issues, I did not include the nine paraeducators with whom I had a direct working relationship. Those paraeducators who did not fall within the guidelines would no doubt have been contributing participants, but I wanted to avoid entering into a dual relationship with them. I did not want to be both their superior in the organization and their lead investigator in research. I wanted them to speak candidly and without concerns that I would use any information that they gave me for research purposes in a work-related context.

With these factors, six paraeducators met all criteria. With six participants, I was able to gather enough data to generate themes through analysis. I met with each potential participant to invite her to take part in the book. All potential participants agreed to engage in the book. In fact, they were eager to tell their story.

Access

As a member of the school child study team in the Water Wheel School, I am in a good position to talk to and participate in the daily work life of the paraeducators who work in the school. I visit classes on a daily basis to observe students and to confer with teachers and paraeducators. I am not a supervisor, but work in an advisory position where I can ask questions and have questions asked of me. Entry into the site was possible, without disturbing the landscape, because I am part of the landscape.

I understand taken-for-granted assumptions because I am an experienced worker at the site. I am an insider. While I am an insider in the school, I fulfill a different role in the hierarchy from the paraeducators. This difference in hierarchy might have posed barriers to communication, but I think that these barriers were overcome by virtue of recruiting participants from the group of paraeducators with whom I did not work, the relationships mutually developed over the course of the interviews and the observations and their desire to be heard.

Chapter 3: A Way of Looking For Answers

Interviews

In the middle of January 2008, I started the series of interviews. I designed the protocols to include a combination of questions to add breadth and depth to the results: experience/behavior, opinion/values,[82] identity [83] and agency [84]. To keep the interviews open, I prepared six to twelve major questions for each interview and then asked probing questions during the interview.

Each participant was interviewed three times for approximately 40 minutes, with each interview five to eight weeks apart over the course of six months. During the first interview, I focused the discussion upon questions of their identity. During the second interview, I asked the participants how they perceive their relationship to the teachers they work with in the general education classrooms. I asked about their relationship with students during the third interview.

I intended that the listed questions for the interviews serve as a guide so that areas of interest for the purpose of this book were explored. The order of questions varied among the eighteen planned interviews depending upon the paraeducator's answers. I requested added detail or explanation during the interviews as seemed appropriate.

The interviews were conducted at the convenience of each paraeducator, before, during or after regular working hours at the school. Sometimes, the interviews lasted longer than the scheduled time of forty minutes due to the participants desire to clarify a point or to continue a discussion.

---

[82] Patton, 1990
[83] Wenger, 1999
[84] Holland, 1998

The Paraeducator: The Other Grown-Up In The Classroom

Observations

While I am very familiar with the research site, I do not look at it through the eyes of the paraeducators. In order to describe the context and create an in-depth description, I accompanied each assistant during one entire workday as well as on five other occasions for a shorter time. I used the fourteen observable signs of a community of practice to frame my observations.[85] These observations were spread out over the course of six months, during the same period as the interviews.

My observations informed my interviews and vice versa. These are formal arrangements that marked the least amount of interaction I had with each participant, and I had many additional opportunities for informal discussions and informal observations.

Informal interactions

Throughout the course of research for this book, I had opportunity for informal observations in the classrooms. I was available to engage in further conversation during the course of the workday. I made notes of casual conversations as soon as possible after the conversation to supplement the scheduled interviews, using a field notebook. I gathered relevant documents such as forms, schedules and memos. I used these documents for the purpose of triangulation, to confirm other evidence and as an additional way to provide context to the paraeducators' work.

Analysis and Presence

Framing a question presupposes philosophical, political and class stances, arising from my identity and role. To bracket my biases from the ideas of the participants, I need to reveal my background

---

[85] Wenger, 1999, p. 125-126

and my place within the school organization. I need to describe myself.

Underlying my time in schools has been my New England up bringing. I imbibed the Transcendentalist belief of education as part politics and part self-improvement. I am female, white, middle aged and since the age of five have gone to school: as a student, as a teacher and as an educational diagnostician with extensive training through graduate study. From this training, I have multiple certificates, including reading teacher, teacher of the handicapped and school psychologist. For the last twenty-four years of my school career, I have been a learning consultant, which is a special education teacher who has received training in achievement and perceptual test administration. I also use these standardized tests to determine students' eligibility for special education and related services. In addition to being a gatekeeper at the entrance to special education, I am one of the experts who form the principal's group of advisors. Through this role, I am positioned alongside the school psychologist, the guidance counselor, and the nurse in the school hierarchy. I spend time in classrooms, observing students and consulting with teachers.

Usually, my relationship with a paraeducator consists of brief discussions in the beginning of the school year about the students with whom the paraeducator will be working, as well as incidental discussions throughout the year. These discussions often take place in the back of a classroom, when they can spare a few minutes while their student or students work independently.

While I can say I collaborate with a paraeducator, our places in the organization are not equal. The paraeducators move from class to class during the day. They have a specific schedule imposed upon them for every period, every minute of the day, while I have the freedom to shape my workday. They have a locker in a workroom in which to place their belongings. In contrast, I have a private office. These differences are the outward manifestations of place in the hierarchy, power and agency.

Limits of the research

A potential limit of this research is that the participants are middle class women who have built-in privilege. From the viewpoint of my research, this status of the participants is not a limit but a plus.

Race, class and cultural differences are constructs that often divide people and have been explored in other studies.[86] If I focus on these constructs, I may obstruct my understanding of paraeducator perceptions-the purpose of this study. During interviews, observations and communications, none of the participants initiated a discussion of the status marker of race or class. This omission might be a sign of participant reticence, rather than lack of the existence of such a marker. Given this potential ambiguity, I set aside these descriptors as status markers, hoping to unearth information that previous research has not been able to uncover about power relationships, psychological issues and other issues of status.

By negating the variables of class, the participants revealed other variables that are key to understanding the role of paraeducator. In using the informal community of practice as the frame through to view their work, rather than the individual paraeducator or the school organization, I describe how a group of people perceives their occupation in this time and in this place.

---

[86] Chopra, et al, 2004;Lewis, 2003;Smith, 2000

Chapter Four
The Setting: Like No Other Place

Geography, History and Population of the Site

New Jersey is divided into counties and within these counties are political entities termed townships. The East Brighton-Fieldtown[87] school district serves the children of two separate townships in an area that was once consisted of rural farms on some of the richest land in central New Jersey. The land is flat, bounded by hedgerows, and one small river. The soil is rich, deep, free of rocks and well drained by the tame Water Wheel Stream. Located midway between the ports of New York and Philadelphia, farmers took produce such as potatoes and pumpkins overland or by waterway for transport to these markets.

East Brighton was first settled in the 18th century by Dutch farmers. Their children attended one-room schoolhouses until 1917 when their descendants built the first of four consolidated, graded schools. The schools were in two separate school districts in the adjoining towns. In 1969, the citizens of the two towns voted to merge into one school district, while keeping their municipal governments separate. Their impetus may have been to save money to build their own high school, for children from both townships were attending high school in neighboring Ivytown. The district high school was completed four years after the merger.

In the 1970's, as pharmaceutical and chemical firms burgeoned in the nearby Route One corridor, housing developers eyed the

---

[87] All place names are pseudonyms or substitutions with the exception of well-known markers, such as New York, Philadelphia and Route One.

38

cleared farmland as ideal building sites. They bought the farms and dug the land for foundations rather than soybeans. The builders made the houses larger in size with each succeeding decade, from modest eighteen hundred square-foot spilt level houses of the seventies to the construction of five thousand plus square-foot two and three story homes between 2000 and 2008. Farmers who own ten large farms continue commercial agriculture by growing strawberries, soybeans, potatoes and pumpkins. They sell some to wholesalers and the others they sell retail through farm stands or through offering "pick your own" fruit and vegetable experiences for the family and local school groups. The writer of the East Brighton website reports that fifty percent of the town's land has been preserved as open space.

Citizen concern for education created Fieldtown, the partner town in the district with East Brighton. In New Jersey, each school district must have voters agree to the school year expenditures through a vote. The town had been part of a nearby village, Blueberry, which had more voters. As town residents have told the story to me, Blueberry built a new graded school in 1914 too far for Fieldtown students to attend. When Fieldtown residents asked for a school for their children, the other town's residents said that it would be unpatriotic to ask for a new building during a war. In reaction, Fieldtown created their own town in order to have their own school district. Fieldtown completed their new school in 1919. The school is still in use, and the children who attend that school in grades kindergarten through three go on to attend fourth and fifth grade at the Water Wheel School. Many of the parents volunteer frequently in the school, continuing that tradition of active civic involvement.

Children from East Brighton join children from Fieldtown in fourth grade at the Water Wheel School. Some of the children

39

share the English names seen on the farm stand signs, but children whose last names are Chinese, Pakistani, Indian, Korean and Japanese join them. The district has changed from rural to suburban in the past twenty years and from farm families of Dutch and English descent to a multi-national mix of families. In 1975, six years after the local school boards created the combined district, four schools enrolled 2518 children. By 1985, a steady increase of slightly less than one hundred children per year resulted in an enrollment of 3400 children. Between 1985 and 1995, the number of children almost doubled to 6400 and the district built three new schools to accommodate them. Ten years later, in 2005, the number of children grew by another 3,000 to 9,400 and the district built three additional schools.

The increase in the total number of children and schools is one aspect of change in the district. The district's academic reputation soared, and with it, house prices and property taxes. With the rise in the socio-economic level, the school district is now considered a "J" level by the state, at the opposite end of the scale from the "A" level Abbott districts of the impoverished inner cities of Trenton, Newark and Camden.[88] While adjusting to an ever increasing population created crowding and the stress of creating new schools, the increase also meant that the district did not have to abide by a state imposed cap on increased spending. Money for personnel increases and new equipment was, in comparison to the surrounding built-out districts, ample.

In addition to the impact of the population increase and the fiscal impact, the children were of racial and ethnic backgrounds new to the district. The townships had been predominantly white, with a seasonal influx during the harvest of African American

---

[88] State of New Jersey, 2009

The Paraeducator: The Other Grown-Up In The Classroom

children whose parents were migrant workers. From teacher recollections and a review of old photographs, the year-round residents would have been about 95% white and 5% African American. Migrant workers started to keep their families in the south in the early 80's, with only the men coming to the township according to a retired teacher. In 1998, parents registering their children for kindergarten self-identified in the following way: 64% of the children were white, 25% were Asian, 7% were African American and 4% were Hispanic. In 2007, parent self-described 57% of the children as Asian, 37% white, 4% African American and 2% Hispanic. Many of the African American and Hispanic children live in the apartments in one area of the township that includes subsidized housing. The Asian children are part of a new majority.

The word "Asian" to describe the new majority is not used as a substitute for Asian-American. The children were not born in the United States, and if they were, many never heard English except on television until they entered school. Most of these families are Asian, from China and India (35%).

Chinese is often heard in the halls of Water Wheel School, and no one turns to stare. Parents often presume that teachers know which section of India speaks Gujarati, Urdu or Kannadu. White children comprise 37% of the population of the school but some of these children are immigrants from Russia, France, England, and Greece.[89]

The people who reside in the two townships represent varying economic strata, although the average family income is above the

---

[89]I use my limited skills as a speaker of French to translate for children suddenly relocated from Paris or Port Au Prince. The principal calls upon anyone with any linguistic ability in anything other than English to help communicate with parents and children.

state average by 7%. While many parents work as upper level managers of corporations, scientists at a nearby university physics laboratory, or as entrepreneurs, some work in the restaurants in the area earning slightly better than minimum wage. The "average" high income covers a huge disparity between the high and low end.

The Mindset of Excellence

Of the ten school buildings the children attend, seven were built within the last 19 years, four of them within a four-year period between 1999 and 2002. Each building was on the cutting edge of design when it was built—the most recent school has a geothermal system for heating and cooling. According to educational professionals outside the district, the district is also lauded for keeping current with the latest techniques in pedagogy. The spelling is a program called Ganske, the writing program is developed and supported by Columbia University and the science is a hands-on kit program called "E=mc^2". If you are a typical student, your SAT scores in your junior year will be 1188.[90] As in Garrison Keillor's fictional Lake Wobegone, all the children are above average.

Personnel from the State of New Jersey Department of Education officially recognized this district as one of the most elite in the state, ranked according to economic and educational factors such as home prices and SAT scores. According to demographic data provided by the state, the children in this district have the highest level of financial resources available in their homes. East Brighton-Fieldtown raises about 80% of its taxes through local levies, and gains about 20%, from the state government, in contrast to its closest

---

[90] State of New Jersey, 2009b

inner-city school district, Rivertown, which has the reverse ratio: 20% from local taxes and 80% from state funding.

The district vies with nearby Ivytown for top honors as the most exclusive and competitive school district in the area. Educators in the area know that the East Brighton-Fieldtown district demands a high level of performance from its employees. The municipal website says: "The East Brighton-Fieldtown Regional School District is a highly-renowned school system.[91]

Most of the children's families moved here within the past ten years due to the excellent schools and the manageable commuting distance to New York. At the time of the study, the 2007-2008 school year, the community experienced brisk sales of existing housing and new construction. The parents are usually both well educated and often deliberately chose to live in the district to provide a good education for their children. Parents have said to me that they "expect the best from *this* school district", and emphasize the word "this".

The district's motto is "where excellence in education is a reality." Taken out of context, that motto may seem like a boast, but the district administration and staff treat it as a matter of fact. In private conversations, staff say: "Is this the best we can do?" By saying the "best we can do", they imply that "good enough" is not acceptable. The school parking lots are filled with teachers' cars hours after the children leave the building. After hours, they meet with each other and gather materials for the next day's lessons. The staff strives to fulfill that motto and parents support their efforts by passing school budgets annually.

---

[91] 96% of the students go on to college, and the district has the 4th highest SAT scores in NJ.

Chapter 4: The Setting: Like No Other Place

According to the East Brighton-Fieldtown Strategic Plan developed in 2006, the committee focused upon individual achievement and individual worth, saying: "students will plan to pursue their personal and educational aspirations." With a nod to community, they look at attaining individual virtues, such as honesty and integrity.

Water Wheel School: Numbers and Statistics

Of the ten schools in the district, four are elementary schools holding grades preschool through three. The high schools have grades nine through twelve; the middle schools have grades six through eight while grades four and five are in either the Borough School or the Water Wheel School. The Borough School serves children from East Brighton, while the Water Wheel School draws most of the children from Fieldtown for their general education classes. Children from both areas attend Water Wheel for specialized programs covering autism, preschool handicaps and cognitive delays, including Down syndrome.

The district published a brochure entitled the "New Jersey School Report Card", in which the administration of the district reports the achievements of the past year to the community. On the page dedicated to the Water Wheel School, the descriptors include "outstanding instrumental and vocal music program", "accelerated and enriched mathematics program", "strong parent-teacher associations", and "creative, productive, enjoyable and humanistic environments". The school has earned numerous awards for academic excellence indicating that the practices in this school may be among the best in the state.

During the 2005-2006 school year, each class contained an average of 21.7 students, exceeding the state average of 19.2. Other statistics demonstrate greater differences between the school

44

and the state average and give a flavor of Water Wheel School: 21.2 % of the students either enter or exit the school during the year, compared to the state average of 11.9%. The percentage of children who received an in-school or out-of-school suspension was 0.1%, opposed to a state wide 4.4%. Despite the high mobility rate, these statistics show that the students do not behave in a manner that elicits strong disciplinary consequences in school.

Water Wheel School: Physical Plant

The school building was constructed in 1990 of red brick and glass, centered in the middle of flat fields, which now surround the building as playing fields on two sides. The middle school is on the south side of the building. Across a four lane street is the northern district high school, completed eight years ago, which is a modern, sleek two-story edifice. Water Wheel is also a long and low but a single story building, with a floor plan that resembles a diamond made of branching fans.

The flagpole at the stone entrance court flies the Stars and Stripes. Beyond the courtyard, the double-door main entrance opens with a swipe key, if you are staff. If you are a parent, you need to press a button to trigger a buzzer attached to an intercom so that the main office secretary can release the lock to let you inside after she has scrutinized you through a security camera.

The eight foot air-lock is capped by a barrel of glass, twenty feet in the air and ten feet high, a three dimensional Palladian turned window. The next set of double doors leads into the twenty-five foot wide main corridor. The main office door is to the left and the library door to the right. As you enter the hall, a 200-gallon aquarium that mimics the Water Wheel stream ecosystem would catch the eye of most visitors. A fifth grade teacher who retired as an industrial biologist before beginning this second career maintains the green murk of plants, logs, eels, turtles and fish.

Early in the morning, just before classes start, usually three or four students laden with huge backpacks, cluster around the tank. They are looking. They are just looking, because they are well-behaved children who can read the small printed request on the front of the aquarium: "Please do not touch the glass or make loud noises. It will frighten the animals."

The hall with twelve-foot ceilings extends past the aquarium to a central intersection with three other corridors, forming a gathering place under several large skylights, twenty feet up. Large cloth room-dividers are in each of the four corners of the area, covered with the children's artwork, each well mounted, matted and labeled by the art teacher. At the beginning of the day, children who walk to school or get rides from their parents gather in this main area.

Like spokes of a wheel, four 20-foot corridors radiate from the common area, each with tall windows with eighteen-inch window ledges made of black slate. The ledges are just the right size for nine and ten year olds to perch upon while hearing a lecture in the hall or looking at the butterfly garden in one of the twelve outdoor courtyards. Each corridor leads to clusters of classrooms, all with high windows letting in natural light. The carpeted hallways muffle the sounds of voices and the width provides plenty of room even at each end of the school day when crowded with children entering and exiting.

A strip of metal, holding corkboard, runs the length of the corridors outside each classroom and is designed to hang posters and completed papers for display. All classrooms hold several computers and a television mounted to the wall, which acts as a computer screen. Several "smart boards" are due to be installed this year. Hardbound books are evident in abundance on the well-stocked shelves. Colorful posters fill the walls, exhorting the students to celebrate diversity or to build character. While every room has the stamp of the individual teacher, most are uniformly generously proportioned, well supplied, clean and neat.

Water Wheel School: The Students

As a group, the students are well behaved, even on their own. In fact, the good behavior of the children is something remarkable. They are not quiet and many dance down the corridors, sometimes backwards, as they talk to friends. They seem to listen, like and respect the adults in the building. Most first time visitors to the school notice the children doing errands on their own, walking through the halls without adult supervision. Vandalism is rare. Every other year or so, in the spring, someone in the fifth grade writes something rather tame on the walls in the boys' bathroom in "A" wing, such as "Mrs. Russo wears short skirts". The assistant principal, the subject Mrs. Russo, usually tracks down the culprit and has him wash it off the wall, or if he used permanent marker, has him repaint the wall. She expects the culprit to make amends and then revert to being a well-behaved member of the school community.

Most students dress like a typical Jersey child—t-shirts, jeans, and sneakers. It is the uniform of boys and girls alike. Before 9/11, some of the male children wore turbans and some of the female children wore shawls over their heads. No one made a rule to outlaw clothes that denote a person's religion. The shawls and turbans just disappeared. In the uncertain months after the World Trade Center attack, perhaps parents wanted to prevent the children from becoming victims of hate crimes. Clothes from their home countries only reappear on school declared festivals about

"America, the melting pot" as part of social studies. On those days, the children wear silk and jewelry and their mothers and grandmothers bring in savory and sweet foods from recipes developed on the other side of the world. In the early part of the school year, some parents or grandparents wait in the common area with a few of these 4th and 5th graders until the doors open for school at 8:30. Usually by November, most of the children have convinced their parents to leave them on their own for the fifteen minutes until 8:45, when they may enter their classrooms because the teachers' early morning planning period ends.

Water Wheel School: The Parents

By self-report, 100% of the families who send children to the school say they speak English in the home, but by my estimate, closer to 35% speak another language as their mother tongue and use that native language in the home. Many of the parents do not have the knowledge of English to speak to the teachers or staff without a translator, who is usually their child. The language barrier can be awkward during a discipline problem with that same child and generally, the teachers who speak Chinese, Japanese, or Spanish help to translate.

Some foreign born parents pursue citizenship status, but many live in the United States with "green card" status from the immigration service, allowing them to work in this country. Their corporate relocation office recommends that they purchase or rent homes in the East Brighton-Fieldtown area, due to the school district's reputation. Many of these parents remain in the Water Wheel School district area for a short stay. Their corporation often transfers them as they finish training or complete their project. As their numbers have increased, there has been a corresponding growth in formal support groups, social clubs and language training institutes for Chinese, Korean, Japanese, Bengali, Gujarati and Urdu speakers.

Parents from other cultures sometimes have difficulty translating the Water Wheel School environment to their own schooling background. The Water Wheel School is casual, with children speaking from wherever they happen to be, whether they are seated in their chair, standing by the pencil sharpener or lying on the floor. They leave for the bathroom down the hall when they feel like it, taking the hall pass and not needing teacher permission.

In contrast, many parents tell me that they stood up in class when they were called upon, faced the teacher, and gave a recitation of memorized information. The emphasis upon problem solving and comprehension is unlike the foreign grammar schools some attended which emphasized rote skill acquisition. Again, unlike the schools that many parents attended, grades are not assigned on report cards until the second quarter of the 4th grade year, and then only for science and social studies.

Despite the lack of formal grades, the teachers do make judgments. Teachers recommend which students should be tested for special education support, basic skills reading and math support and gifted and talented programs. Despite the informality and kindness toward the children, which seems to make some of the foreign educated parents doubt the rigor of the education when compared to their own, the teachers are carefully weighing the children's achievement and potential. The American born and educated parents are in the minority at the school, yet, unlike their foreign born counterparts, they are the parents who have a disproportionate share of the vote on the school budget. They are citizens with voting rights. The town natives are in the minority but many are vocal and involved in the volunteer fire department, school board, zoning board and other civic duties.

Another outlet for voicing opinions about the school district is the unofficial parent maintained website called "East Brighton Today". Six years ago, one disgruntled parent from East Brighton started this website and list service on which she gives her opinion of teachers, by name. She also lists hints on how to get a child into the desired gifted programs, even if he or she had not qualified through the school sorting process. She lists names of administrators to contact, and a script of what to say. While Fieldtown parents did not initiate the service, some do use it and they quote from postings on it to the principal. The administrators in charge of the building seem to have a full day's work.

Water Wheel School: Administrators and Office Staff

The principal is a middle aged white woman whose demographics match the majority of the teachers she leads. The 100 teachers, paraeducators, support staff and administrators who make up the faculty and staff of the school are overwhelmingly white, middle aged and female. These demographics are very different from the changing demographics of the district students, and more closely reflect the district demographics of twelve years ago.

She and the assistant principal are women who taught for years before they became guidance counselors. Anna Abrams, the principal, stands six feet tall, and she can command attention with just a few words using a booming voice. She maintains attention because she is bright, knowledgeable and a person with a great wit and a sense of fun. I do not want to portray her one-dimensionally because she expresses her awareness of the complex and contradictory crosscurrents in the school. The school assistant principal, Suzanne Russo is also a person with great wit and understanding.

These administrators give every impression that they love their jobs and the school reflects their attitude. They expect their staff to use real judgment during the course of the day and convey optimism that the staff is doing as well as humanly possible under the circumstances. If any adult sees a child who needs help, that adult is expected to assist that child. Anna makes it clear that support staff, in which category she includes herself, exist to help the teachers do their jobs. The principal gives teachers clout. A number of teachers have transferred to this building specifically to work with her.

I have heard it said that a kind doctor needs a tough nurse at the front desk. The Water Wheel School follows the same model. The head secretary puts up "with no guff" as she is fond of saying. She plays the "bad guy" to the principal's "good guy" and tries to control the flow of people in an out of the principal's office. Two other secretaries are in the front office and they work as a threesome to give feedback to the staff, students and parents. Like a Greek chorus, they comment on the behavior of everyone who passes through the main office.

Water Wheel School: The Teachers

While the children's demographics have changed, the demographics of the staff have remained stable, due to low turnover. Of the thirty-six classroom teachers, only one teacher left her job last year, and that was to follow her husband to California, when he was given a promotion. The teachers are not the highest paid in the county, but are in the middle range for salaries. They receive comprehensive medical benefits. The school district also provides excellent educational benefits: for the teachers, the district pays for all tuition, fees and books for twelve graduate credits per year at any college and university.

Twenty percent of the faculty members are taking graduate level courses this school year according to the district head of personnel. Maintaining and exceeding a reputation takes effort beyond the regular hours of the job, and this exceeding the expected may be one of "certain styles recognized as displaying membership" in this community of practice.[92]

The Water Wheel School: The Paraeducators

There are twenty-two paraeducators working in the Water Wheel School. The children to whom they are assigned may have behavioral problems in addition to academic concerns. Twelve work exclusively in self-contained special education classes with children who have autism, cognitive delays, or moderate learning disabilities. This research does not include them. The remaining ten work for the majority of their day in general education classrooms with targeted students. I work directly with four of the ten, so they, too, are not included in the research. The identity and membership in the community of practice of the remaining six guided the data collection. I have arranged their stories by their time working in the school building, and when both had the same amount of time, by age. First, there is Pat.

[92] Wenger, 1999, p. 126

Chapter Five
Pat Jacobs
A Step on the Ladder

Pat's Story of Self-identification

Pat is twenty-six, tall, blond and with a strong muscular build. She moves with a self-assured athletic bounce to her step that reminds me of the Celtics basketball player, Larry Bird. Not surprisingly, she tells me that she played basketball all through college and planned to be a coach. After college, she continued her education by enrolling in a master's program in athletic administration while working as an assistant coach with the women's college basketball team.

She interrupted the master's degree at one college to take an assistant coaching job at another, but she was not hired permanently. Blocked there, she revised her career plans and she decided to try high school coaching instead. She would like to be an athletic director of a high school, but she needs five years teaching experience for that position. With that in mind, she planned to get certified to teach physical education. The head of human resources in the school district, Alison Gretchick, advised her that job openings for physical education teachers are scarce. Pat used that information to again revise her plan. Now, she is thinking of entering a certification program at a local college to become a language arts teacher.

"At this point, I'm stepping on my own toes just trying to get to where I need to be. Right now, I have like eight jobs. I work here. I coach field hockey in the fall, I coach JV [junior varsity] girls' basketball. I'm also a personal trainer, exercise specialist. I was working three years at the fitness center in Securities Investment Corporation in Goodwater. So I work there part time and I also work at our company called Add One. We're also in the Wyndham Hotel right here off of Grant's Mill Road up in Fieldtown. I'm also a lifeguard. I do that in the summer. I also do one-on-one basketball training, my own personal training."

She explains why she worked so many jobs: "I have a condo in Ginger Farms and I pay a mortgage. Wouldn't want that being taken away or anything. You know, car payments and every other bill in the world. Luckily, I didn't have any student loans to pay cause I got a basketball scholarship for part of it and my mom supplied the other money." In her self-story, Pat looks at where she is, her actual identity and casts that against several future possibilities. The unhappiest possibility would be her losing her home and car. To avoid that designated identity, she focuses on another future identity: becoming an employed teacher.

Towards that end, she is looking for money to pay tuition for her language arts certification. "With instructional assistants", she says, "the district only pays three credits for the year. Teachers or full time get twelve credits for the year. I mean, it is what it is." She does not complain about the disproportionate benefit. " For me to get a job, I'm just going to have to take out loans. My mom says she'll put it on her home equity if she has to [get her tuition money]." She laughs ruefully: "You know my goal right now is to apply and take my Praxis in English and then take two or three classes in the summer and fall. Then hopefully I can teach the next year. That's my plan."

Pat changes plans to adapt to circumstances. Her job as an instructional assistant is part of what she needs to do to get where she wants to be, mirroring her on-going formation of her identity.[93] The occupation of paraeducator is a way station for her. "It's not like it's a position that I don't want to be in or took it thinking 'hopefully, I'm going to get out of here soon'. But I always have a lot of plans: to get into the district, get certified at Walker [a local college], to become a teacher. And keep coaching. I can enjoy everything." Enthusiasm radiates from her as she speaks. I realize she coaches herself through her life.

Pat related that this year is her first as a paraeducator and her first year in this school building. She secured the job through her sister: "Currently my sister teaches at the middle school. She's a special ed teacher for sixth and seventh grade. She's been there seven years or so now. She had always wanted to be a teacher and my mom said to me: 'so you should get your teacher certificate.' So my sister Micky suggested that I become an instructional assistant in the district. Obviously, East Brighton is one of the best districts in the county, in addition to the fact that there was a JV [junior varsity] girls coaching position, too. Eventually, I'm looking to be a head coach. And when I came in and interviewed with Kate Spinnings [supervisor of special education], she was like, basically: 'Oh, I know who we're putting you with. I know. This kid needs structure. You can make sure you're on top of him.' She's a former college basketball player, too. She said that I was a personal trainer and I could be strict and I would be tough. But there's a lot of different factors going in, apparently, that they wanted me specifically with this child."

Pat talks about the mesh between her perceived personal capacity and the needs of the community of practice she was entering. She knew a few of the reasons she was considered a good

---

[93] Sfard and Prusak, 2005

fit, which had to do with the characteristics of the targeted student. Some of the characteristics she feels were apparent to her supervisor, while unknown to her. While she has some social connections with teachers in the district through coaching, she does not live in the district, or have children, or children who attend the school system. Having a college degree and working toward attaining a teaching certificate were more important points in her life story.

Several themes emerged from her story. She plans to attain a higher status within the school hierarchy and she ascribes a higher status to her coaching work both in the past and currently than to her paraeducator work. Being a paraeducator is a temporary occupation for her, as is being a teacher. Through the story she tells herself, her self-discourse, she identifies herself as hardworking, ambitious and flexible. I see her as focused, strong and self-assured. I wondered how she would translate that identity as a member of the classroom community of practice.

Pat in the Classroom

I am walking into Peter Bergen's science class at the beginning of seventh period, the next to last period of this January day, to see Pat at work. She is assigned as a one-to-one with a student who came up from the third grade school with a reputation for not doing his schoolwork and physically assaulting fellow classmates. He is known as big, mean, argumentative and a bully. I wonder which of these children is Jack.

Pat is talking to Peter about how close they are to completing a project. In marker on the class white board, the teacher printed: "Do heavy things fall faster than light ones?" Pat seats herself at one of the clusters of desks around the room where three children who are endeavoring to answer the question on the board. Each child has a penny, a feather, a pencil and a printed sheet of paper on his or her desk that are specific tools for this project.

At one of the desks sits a very large redheaded boy. I am correct in deciding that this is Jack. Jack was retained in kindergarten so he is also a year older than the other children. Two other boys, diminutive in contrast to him, sit at the other two desks. Only twelve children appear in a class today that usually holds twenty-six, but I see Peter's schedule on the bulletin board saying that the orchestra rehearses this period. Fourteen of the students are out and assuming that no one is out sick, they are with the music teacher.

Pat says: "You guys have all the same hypothesis?" The three boys nod. "What else did Mr. Bergen say?" No one answers. "Jack?" The tall red headed boy answers: "To record." "That's what Mr. Bergen said. Good, Jack. You are going to do the experiment and then you are going to record the results." Pat reviews what the children should know by referencing the teacher, showing her view of her place in the school hierarchy. She also shows that she knows the specific tools the students need to do their work, a sign of membership in a community of practice.[94]

Jack watches one of his partners drop a penny and a feather from his desktop and then writes on his paper. Jack then drops his feather and penny while the other two students watch. The two boys start to talk about who has the faster penny and who has the faster feather. Pat says: "You need to do some more. Mr. Bergen wants you to establish a baseline. He said to 'focus on the procedures' remember?" Pat keeps them on the path to satisfactory completion of the lab report by referring, again, to what the teacher has said. By aligning herself with the teacher's authority, she

---

[94] Wenger, 1999

shows that they share a way of doing things together, which is both further evidence of a community of practice and her membership within it.[95]

I watch Peter Bergen walking around the room and stopping to talk to each of the three other groups of children in the room about their experiments. He spends about five or six minutes with each group. He eventually gets to the group where Pat is working and spends only three minutes with them. I wonder if the students, in gaining Pat's help, forfeit a portion of the teacher's attention.

Peter comes over to where I am sitting by the back of the room to tell me about his class procedures. He is a tall, muscular man, who with his back to the class, blocks my view of Pat and her students. He is explaining that he checks the students' homework daily and sets up the first assignment of the day for the students. He interacts with me as if I am there to look at a student's program, my usual role in classrooms. I cannot evade his perception of me as a child study team member. Despite my concern that I am being distracted from what I want to see, I appreciate the positive side of my dilemma, that my role helps me blend into the community of practice.

As he shows me the log the children are filling out, I hear Pat speaking loudly the words: "Jack, focus!" And then she says: "Mr. Bergen? I've told Jack to take that off his head." I can now see that in the 60 seconds that Peter Bergen has had his back to the class, Jack took a turtle shell that from a nearby shelf and put it on his head. "Off?" she says. Peter takes a minute to give Jack a long glare. When Jack does not remove the shell, Peter says: "Take that shell off your head." Jack takes it off and puts it back on the shelf. Pat looks relieved and makes a joke out of the incident, saying:

---

[95] Ibid.

"Got to take that off, causing brain waves not to escape. And you need the brain power." Pat expresses her irritation with him using a joke, under Mr. Bergen's watchful eye. Jack says nothing in reply. This story illustrates Wenger's ninth observable sign of a community of practice: "the ability to assess the appropriateness of actions and products" as well as knowing what others can do.[96] In this sequence of actions and reactions, Pat again demonstrates direction through referral to another power. I am surprised by her indirect approach to discipline of this student because I do not think it reflects the persona she conveyed in our interview when she was talking about Kate Spinnings expectation that she would be structured and tough. Even in casual conversations in the hall, she conveyed decisiveness and action.

Pat looks at Jack's paper and says directly: "This is too hard to read." Jack replies: "I can read it fine. Why do *you* need to read it?" Pat rejoins quickly: "So I could read it and duplicate it." Peter Bergen overhears the conversation and says: "Exactly. To be able to read it and do it." Pat gets Jack to do what she wants, but she shows care to avoid confrontation. She calls on an outside locus of control, either the need of Science and/or the teacher, rather than taking personal responsibility for her unwelcome directives. Her teacher is on the alert to support her with Jack, and they have been working with Jack and with each other for five months. I wonder if either her authority is still tenuous, or Jack habitually bucks authority. He seems to enjoy attracting the attention of everyone in the classroom. She is so verbally quick with him that I admire her fast thinking on her feet, but doing this all day, every day (and children like Jack, in my experience, rarely spend a day at home out of school) looks exhausting.

---

[96] Wenger, 1999, p.125

Chapter 5: Pat Jacobs A Step On The Ladder

The teacher comes over to their group and refocuses the group on the task: "I'm not sure knowing the grams will help you with the experiment. What is your hypothesis?" None of the three volunteers an answer. Pat prompts Jack: "Do you want to read *your* hypothesis?" Jack likes the attention and reads his hypothesis. Peter Berger starts to tell the three boys about a short cut to getting the information they need. Pat joins in the conversation, reiterating what the teacher says with: "Maybe you want to use the thing whose mass you know?" I realize that she is framing much of what she says as a suggestion.

Once the boys are working, Pat asks Peter: "How are the kids in orchestra going to get this done?" He tells her that they will just have to copy the information from the children who have stayed in class. While I know she does not need to do this for Jack, she is being helpful both to the students who have orchestra and their homeroom teacher. By posing this question, she shows evidence of belonging to a community of practice through quickly setting up a problem to be discussed and the rapid flow of information she and the teacher exchange.[97] She resolved this ambiguity through discourse with the science teacher, showing evidence of another component of conceptual framework of this study.[98]

Pat relies on the teacher for authority when Jack violates the behavior mores for students. While I saw her convey the energy and social adeptness of her interview into her role in the classroom, I was surprised to see her temper her directness with caution. Perhaps that caution derives from her understanding of Jack's oppositional personality and a well-crafted approach to working with him. She creates a position as a reminder of authority, not an

---

[97] Wenger, 1999.
[98] Connell, 2002

60

The Paraeducator: The Other Grown-Up In The Classroom

embodiment of authority. Indeed, during another observation, I saw further evidence of her carefully created classroom role.

Four months later in May, I revisit Pat. At 8 a.m. that day, I see the teacher, Maureen O'Malley, already working at her desk. The sun, bouncing off the ceiling from the wall of huge windows, bathes the colorful posters on the walls that say: "Character Counts", "Ask Three before me", and "Happy Birthday". A bulletin board illustrates the school's writing program, the "Writer's Workshop".

Pat enters the room quickly, pulling off a long sweater and hanging it in the closet in the back of the room. She asks Maureen about the previous day with: "How did comp go without us yesterday?" "Comp" seems to stand for computer class. "Okay," says Maureen without taking her eyes off the computer screen. "What today?" Pat rejoins. Maureen's reply: "Level papers, on the computer". Pat and Maureen have no introductory preamble as if they are engaged in an on-going conversation, which is another piece of evidence that they are mutually engaged in a community of practice.[99] Pat explains to me what their personal jargon means. She tells me that it is not going to be a "typical day" because there will be two periods of language arts, so the students will be improving their papers, that is, bringing them up to the next level through an editing process they have been taught on the computers. Jargon is another sign of the existence of a community of practice.[100]

She and Maureen discuss the day in terms of Jack's needs. He may not be in a good mood because the whole social studies lesson with Tori Green, who is one of Maureen's two co-teachers, is going to be based upon homework. Jack rarely does homework.

[99] Wenger, 1999
[100] Ibid.

Chapter 5: Pat Jacobs A Step On The Ladder

The way Pat said this was compressed: "He's not going to be in a good mood. Didn't do social studies, got nothing". Their form of speech is so abbreviated, it seems like a code to me. Maureen just nods and leaves the room. These short exchanges of information using insider phrases are more evidence of a shared community of practice.[101]

Maureen brings in a second metal cart on wheels, and several students follow her into the room. The children say: "Cows!" in unison. Their teacher agrees that they will be working on the COWS this morning. Maureen explains to me that these are the Computers on Wheels. Maureen leaves the room again and Pat directs the students with: "OK, guys, unpack." She sets out the computers, three on each side of the room for each cluster of desks and one for her student to use. Others will share, but Jack has his own. Pat's presence confers this special privilege on him, an anomaly in the usual procedures in this classroom.

A child comes up to Pat to complain about a group member's behavior. Pat goes to the accused one and says: "Monique, are you helping? You look like you're playing around with the pencil. I want to make sure that everybody's involved." The offender says: "Why?" as a challenge, but Pat ignores her and walks away. In walking away from a potential confrontation, Pat has duplicated the behavior I observed in January. She did not engage in the power struggle, whose point for the student would be to emphasize her power and Pat's lack. Maureen witnesses the interchange, and shoots Monique a cautionary look. Monique stops challenging Pat, now that the teacher intervenes. The participants in this exchange demonstrate their understanding of their mutually defining identities that serves as further evidence of their membership in a

---

[101] Wenger, 1999.

community of practice.[102] They also demonstrate that Pat's position is less than the teacher's in the classroom hierarchy, but greater than the student's.

Pat and Maureen walk around the classroom and encourage each student. After every other student in the class seems to be writing, Pat sits down beside Jack. She likes what Jack is doing and says to Maureen: "Hey, Miss O., check this out." Maureen looks at Jack's work. Pat has asserted her status by doing work with the teacher and also gaining positive attention for her student.

At 10:15, Pat and the students move to Tori Green's classroom next door for social studies, leaving Maureen behind in her room to teach math to Tori's students. The two classes pass in the hallway. Pat enters Tori's class and sits in the back of the class as Tori begins the class.

The children and Tori engage in a discussion of voting rights springing from their recent field trip to the historic sights in Philadelphia. She calls on a student, but gets her name wrong. Tori teaches in a "triple", a group of three classes in which three teachers exchange students for science, math and social studies. This grouping reduces the preparation work she needs to do but it also gives her seventy-seven names to remember. Pat supplies the correct name, quickly and quietly. She fills in the gap in Tori's memory discretely. Their sustained mutual relationship shows their engagement in a joint enterprise.[103]

Pat discusses with Tori the need for the adults in the classroom to divide the students into pairs. "Partnerwise" she says. Tori prefers to have the children choose their own partners. She confers further with Pat who tells her that Jack might be left out if the students choose their own partner. Tori is persuaded to change her

---

[102] Ibid.
[103] Wenger, 1999.

plan. She decides to use a counting strategy to partner the students. Pat uses persuasion and recommendation to prevent social difficulties for Jack.

Jack gets a partner, who does not look pleased. The partner says impatiently: "Jack, come on" when Jack does not move quickly. Pat defends his slowness to his classmate saying: "He's just putting away scissors." Pat seems quick to defend Jack or perhaps just quick to head off a possible confrontation between the two children. Pat could handle this problem many other ways, but she elects to serve as a buffer and mediator.

By eleven o'clock, the class ends, and the children return to their homeroom before heading to the cafeteria. Pat tells me that she is on duty during lunch and sits with a group of girls, near Jack, who is at a separate table with other boys.

In the cafeteria, the girls at Pat's table have brought lunches from home. They are eating and talking while the students in line for hot food go slowly by. Pat is in earnest discussion with the girls. She tells me later that the girls are being "catty and cliquish." As they go out to the playground, she notices a new lunchroom aide. She introduces herself to the newcomer, and shakes the woman's hand. She lets her know that she is with Jack, and who Jack is, welcoming her into the community of practice. On the playground, she circles the area, throws a stray ball back to the group and then sits with a cluster of four adults who are out supervising the playground.

On this beautiful day, the students are running around the blacktop and climbing the playground equipment. Recess passes quickly. One lunchroom aide blows a whistle several times, which signals the children to stop their play. The children line up to reenter the building, and Maureen meets them. She and Pat exchange information as they walk towards the classroom. Pat updates Maureen on students' conversations and activities occurring out of her classroom. Pat's day is half over. I thank her for letting me shadow her and we set up our time for our next interview. I now have context for Pat's stories about her role in the general education classroom.

Pat's Process of Membership In The Classroom

Based upon her understanding of the community of practice in the classrooms in which she works, Pat exercises social judgment to guide her actions.

Observe

Pat is an observer of Jack's behavior. She knows that Jack notices and chafes at restrictions and control. In response, she calibrates the amount and the kind of help she can give him to avoid irritating him while still having him conform to teacher expectations. Sometimes, she believes that the best she can do for her student is to do very little: "One day in social studies, they ended up doing presentations. There wasn't really anything for me to do. I'll get up if I see him looking around. I'll be sitting in the back of the room, and he will end up just staring at me. And I'll be: 'Don't look at me. I'm not the teacher. Turn around.' Probably better for him that there are down times. Not have me as a crutch. Some days, it's like: 'Miss Jacobs, Miss Jacobs, Miss Jacobs.' 'Okay, what do you need?' I point him in the right direction and then let him do it."

Pat says that she reacts to what she sees as the needs of others. "I observe to see what's what. If there are papers being passed out, let me jump up and pass out half the papers. Or if a teacher is instructing a lesson, or giving directions and I'm not sure, I'll ask clarification questions. Because I know that if I'm not sure, my child is not sure. Or, if I know that it is something my child will start an argument about, saying: 'Oh, Mr. Bergen didn't say that', I will say: 'Mr. Bergen, does this apply here? Should they be putting this in their note book?' 'Oh, yeah, they should be putting this in their note book, this is going to be on the test.' So, I'm just observing until I feel that I am needed or that I can do something." She reacts to others in the community of practice, making choices within limits.

Communicate

Pat converses with the other members of the community of practice for many purposes, including clarifying her understanding and her student's understanding of teacher expectations. "I will go over to Maureen, Tori, Peter, whatever and say: 'Will you go over to Jack and say that this is what needs to be done, because he is not listening to me?' I'll walk off to the side and then they will go over and say what needs to be done. And if he does it then, great. And if he doesn't, well then that's his decision." Pat exhibits discretion to avoid social embarrassing Jack and the potential problems Jack might create in reaction to public correction.

She is not only the initiator of conversation, but also the recipient of support from her teacher through discussions. Maureen guides her through discourse during the workday. "Maureen and I are trying to get to the point where we tell him, he makes the decision and if he doesn't, then he suffers whatever consequences there are. I can't sit there and say: 'You had this reading project.' 'Well, what do I need to do? I don't know what to do.' And I get him on track, give him the cues and he sits there and stares and says: 'I forgot dat…dat..dat…dah.' I say: 'Go back try it again.' Maureen's like: 'You told him. Just go sit down. Let him do it. If he doesn't do it, that's what he hands in.' So, I go sit down, and he realizes, okay, I'm not going to push." She and Maureen talk about how they plan to work with Jack, serving as Pat's mentor and guide. She believes that she walks a fine line between enabling and supporting.

Pat characterizes her job as varied and dependent upon factors beyond her control. "In some classes, I might be able to be more hands on and more able to assist the teacher, and just the daily class activities. Mr. Bergen is strictly lecture some days and some days we are doing experiments. So, it really depends on what we are doing that day, where my child might need more assistance, less assistance."

She discusses what she and the teachers have concluded about Jack's personality and social needs. "He's got to do work and he's got to learn what the consequences for not doing work is. So, now we're trying: 'If you have a good morning and if you do your work and if you're productive and not argumentative, we're going to give you a ticket.' They get tickets for rewards. Different rewards for each certain amount. 'In the afternoon, you'll get a ticket in the afternoon.' That was seeming to work. But there were days last week that we didn't give him any tickets. And I asked him, 'How did you think you did this morning?' 'I think I did ok,' he said. 'Jack, are you sure? Do you think you were good in social studies? Well, how many tickets do you think you should get today?' He did not admit that his behavior had not been good." His behavior is the subject of discussions between the teacher Maureen and Pat as they try to teach him how to be socially appropriate in the classroom.

She does a verbal assessment of Jack's behavior. "Does he want to be aggressive with people? Yes, sometimes. Is he stubborn? Yes. But, it's a learning process everyday. I can't just learn [how to work with him] in twenty-four hours. You see how the kid reacts, you try to judge how you speak to him, how you go about things. It's an everyday process learning what works and what doesn't work."

Pat takes direction from the teacher through discourse, a social interaction. Her discussions with Jack and with his teachers as well as her discussions with the teachers about academic and social expectations are part of her work in the elementary school classroom.

Commit

Pat made a choice to work with Jack and his teachers and keeps that commitment of affiliation throughout the year. Pat talks about the positive aspects of her job: "I enjoy it and it's a good way to almost be on the outside and observe in a classroom while still being in it. And getting a feel: 'Can I do this? Yeah, sure. I can teach fourth grade. I can teach in general.' And you know, seeing how other teachers work. I get to be in at least three different regular classrooms with the social studies, the math and the science switching throughout the day. Then, going to PE [physical education], music and art and seeing the different things that teachers use to grade students. In one of the classrooms she gives points for talking or listening or cleaning up and things like that. Each table gets a point and she adds them up at the end and the winners get something special. It's a good way to prepare; maybe someday maybe I'll have a classroom. Hopefully."

Her loyalty extends to all three teachers who teach Jack. "Sometimes I help out one of the team teachers. Tori's had some doctor appointments in the morning." Pat is discrete and does not elaborate on Tori's medical problem. I know from other sources that the teacher, at the beginning of a high-risk pregnancy, requires frequent visits to the doctor for monitoring. "So I help out in her classroom until maybe nine o'clock, when she gets there." Pat has a substitute-teaching certificate, so she can legitimately be in charge of a class if a teacher is absent. Paraeducators without such a certificate were not supposed to be left alone in the room with children. "I have relationship with the twenty-three kids in her class, too. They know who I am. I tell them to slow down. Or walk, when they are running in the halls." In these two examples, she envisions herself as a placeholder for a teacher. Her flexibility in temporarily performing the teacher's job is useful and convenient for the community of practice and helps her fulfill she defines as her central task: to build a working relationship with the teachers and the students.

Adapt

Pat sees herself as the person who handles the problems with her targeted student until the teacher needs to step in. She treats the teachers as the experts and believes that they have more authority than she. She says: "For me, if Jack is refusing to do something that I think is necessary for his academic achievement or development, I feel bad at some points, because I might be interrupting, but I will stop and say: 'Mr. Bergen, is this something? What do you think about this?' Just because I don't think that Jack always sees me as the highest authority. He thinks he can step over me, or push me around or say: 'No, no, no. This is fine.' Well, it's not. My job is to make sure you are doing the right thing," she addresses Jack rhetorically. She is aware of her imposition on the teacher, but does not presume that she alone is responsible for Jack.

She does believe that her job includes getting Jack to do "the right thing." She knows the right thing through her membership in the community of practice and she measures her success in her job upon her ability to elicit his appropriate behavior. She and Jack have a sustained mutual relationship, sometimes harmonious and sometimes conflicted, is a sign of engagement in a community of practice. It is also a testament to her adaptibility.[104]

Pat envisions herself in a relationship with all the members of the classroom community of practice that is analogous to a family-member relationship. "I guess I am a liaison between the teacher and the student. I sit at a lunch table with some of the girls. I find out before she does, type of thing. I'm the sister-in-the-family kind of thing."

She characterizes herself as a person with derived authority again. Implied, but not stated, was the position of the teacher as the parent in the family. Her words reflect what I saw in the classroom. Evidenced by her behavior and the behavior of the teachers and the students, her rank in the community of practice is below a teacher and above a student, so she can serve as a bridge between the two. Her "bridge" position is being a part, but not always the leader or the focal point, of social interchange.

She explains that she spends more time with the children than Maureen does, either in other teacher's classrooms or in the cafeteria for lunch and on the playground for recess. She says bluntly that she is assigned to the lunchroom with Jack for one reason: "I'm there so he doesn't beat anybody up." But she does not sit with him, again avoiding an appearance of control and potential for direct confrontation.

She continues her social theme: "I'm Maureen's policewoman. We tell the kids: 'Are you telling on somebody, are you being a tattletale or are you giving us information?' But *I* have to be a tattletale. Because I see it and it's not something they're supposed to do so, I see it and tell her."

---

[104] Wenger, 1999.

"I sit in a position where I'm with four of the girls at lunch, and they like it. They like talking to me. I sit in a spot where Jack is where I can see him, because he doesn't need me on top of him. I might see something. I'm with these kids twenty-four seven. So, if I see something going on, if I see notes passing or girls being extra catty or something being said. I might mention it to Maureen. 'Hey, this is something that's going on maybe you can talk to them.' So, you have to teach them social things, too. How to be appropriate." She gave an example: "When we are transitioning from one room to another, all of them. It's like: 'Come on guys, can't you be quiet? Shh! Can't you keep our hands off the wall?' "

Her relationship with the students holds potential ambiguity. She could hold what they say to her in confidence. She resolves this problem through a story of discourse with the teacher that confirms her role as telling the teacher "everything". Tellingly, she does not discipline the students herself. She takes a deliberate, nuanced position between the teacher and students, being neither one nor the other, but serving as a social monitor of student behavior.

Partner

"You have to establish a good working environment. My sister's been teaching for six or seven years and there have been plenty of people that she's had to work on teams with that either didn't like her or she didn't like them for whatever reason. But you have to work together because you are here in a school teaching kids and you have to figure out what works." She established the social aspect of her workplace relationships through discourse. "In the beginning of the day, we [Maureen and she] are both there. I get there some minutes before the kids come in and we chitchat about things. And some times walking down the hall at the end of the day, we get other things in. She's in a couple of singing groups and she tells me about that. We get to have personal conversations. It's not just about school. I know about her husband. Talked to her when her mom died. When you work around people you build relationships. Ask how they're doing. It makes a difference. It's very helpful."

During class, she reports that she talks with Maureen. For example, before she helps some of the students she explains that: "I'll talk to Maureen about it and say: 'Hey, do you want me to check half of theirs? I will ask before I go ahead and take over something. And you know, I talk with Maureen every day. 'Okay, this is what he's done, what can you suggest, if he's not listening to me?' I'll go up to either Peter or Tori in the other classes and say: 'He's not doing this. Can you please go by and say: 'Hey, can you work on this? Because it's not working coming from me, it's probably going to work coming from you.' I'm their hands-on to help him and to guide him, but if he's not listening to me, I got to bring somebody higher in, keep bringing somebody else in. That's my strategy. Go to the next level."

She defined that next level as the teachers, her source of authority. "This is what we're telling you, this is what Mrs. O'Malley's telling you. It's coming from the same person. Just reminding them about the level of the higher level of the chain." Pat sees herself as a person who assists the teachers in their work with Jack. In the classroom, she notes "we definitely collaborate with what we are doing, but it's more like Maureen is supervising over me to see the well-being of this child. She might say: 'You did what you've got to do. Leave him alone.'"

Summary

Pat reveals her identity through discourse about her past, her present and hopes for the future. She narrates a story of her identity by talking about her present role and herself in the future in a designated identity.[105] She is working as a paraeducator which is one of "about eight jobs" she holds presently as a stepping stone to become an athletic director of a school district. She references the teachers when she identifies herself several times as "their hands-on", or "assistant." When she talks about the advantages of the job, she notes that she is *seeing* some good teaching techniques, not that she is *using* some good techniques. She sees teaching and teachers as something she aspires to do and to be, rather than something she is doing currently.

Pat attributes her learning to perform the job through her background experience in other jobs. She never discusses formal training. When asked about how she does her job, she went right to discussing relationships. She says she needs to establish a good working relationship with staff, teachers and students.

She assesses her success in her role by how well her assigned student, Jack, meets teacher expectations. Although she derives satisfaction from fulfilling the role, she judges her personal success upon meeting her financial needs and furthering her career. Her sense of commitment is or one school year, or until she can secure a teaching position. Her tight self-control when her student exhibits oppositional or defiant behavior attests to the social nature of her role within the classroom and to the adaptations she makes within the classroom.

I recorded many instances of Pat's involvement in a community of practice according to Wenger's criteria.[106] Within three classrooms, Pat demonstrates membership in a community of practice. I link community of practice with her social skills, including her observations, communication, commitment and

---

[105] Sfard and Pruzak, 2005.
[106] Wenger, 1999.

adaptability. Through membership in a community of practice, she creates her role that is one possible response to the setting, given her self-identity.[107] She views the role as adaptive. What she does is dependent upon the other people she works with, both teachers and students. Daily, Pat asserts her position between teachers who have authority over her and a student who opposes anyone having authority over him. She maintains this delicate balance through becoming a channel for authority, rather than an authority herself. She builds her place in the community of practice, somewhere between being a teacher and being a student.

She communicates to accomplish several goals. First, she establishes a way to create mutual understanding of expectations with both teachers and students. She talks daily to Maureen about their common work and expectations for Jack. These discussions enable them to avoid misunderstandings in the daily logistics of how to instruct the children. In addition, she and Maureen talk about topics of mutual interest separate from their roles in the community of practice. She builds relationships with both the teachers and the students through daily discussions. Through discourse with teachers and students, she clarifies expectations, gains and gives information on academic work and creates social bonds. She does not confine her discourse to work with the one child assigned to her, but helps the teacher gather materials and solve social problems in the classroom between children other than her targeted child. She resolves ambiguity by talking with the teachers and the students. Discourse is the means by which she adapts to the ongoing process of change and development in the classroom.

---

[107] Connell, 2002.

The Paraeducator: The Other Grown-Up In The Classroom

After being hired, she reports, she received very little job training in a formal sense, beyond specific clarification of logistics. The teachers assumed that Pat already know what to do in general, but not exactly how they, the teachers, want a particular task executed on a particular day with this particular student. Observation, coupled with her communication, enabled her to fashion a position within the classrooms and to partner with the teachers, and on occasion, with the students.

Other people, given the same circumstances, may have fashioned a different persona in the role. Given different circumstances, Pat herself might have fashioned a different persona. Her views of herself are complex and fit into her perception of the capacity and expectations of other people in her community of practice, echoing Reich's assertion that identity is multifaceted.[108]

The next paraeducator, Tiffany, also sees herself as a person who is doing the job for now.

---

[108] Reich, 1991.

Chapter Six
Tiffany Washington
For Now

Tiffany's Story of Self-identification

Tiffany, pretty as her name, has sparkling brown eyes and petite features. She smiles with her whole face and usually looks as if she is barely holding back a laugh. When she does laugh, which occurs often, she giggles softly. She is about five feet tall. She walks fluidly but slowly, because she is a woman of generous proportions. At thirty, she could pass for twenty-two. The first thing she wants me to know is that she is a displaced person.

She and her husband are from the South: "He's a little country boy. So he grew up outside of Mobile and I grew up in Mobile. I'm the city person." She would like to return to the South to be near her family. "I got married and we moved up here. And got *stuck* up here." She emphasizes the word "stuck" and pauses. "My husband was doing his masters at Ivytown Theological Seminary. He had one more year to go. We were just supposed to be up here a year." She pauses again. "And then he got a church. So that's how we got stuck." She says the last three words in a rapid staccato for emphasis.

Their three year old daughter is the only grandchild on both sides of the family "so I hear it once or twice a month: 'Oh, how could you leave me?' My mom, my dad... 'It's the only grandbaby, blah, blah, blah.' So, I try to get down as much as I can."

She feels that her family influenced her to avoid teaching as a career. "Just about everyone in my family is a teacher. Special ed teacher, math teacher, substitute teacher, some type of teacher. From my grandmother, sisters. Everybody. I was trying to get away from teaching." She entered Alabama State as an engineering major.

"And then engineering didn't agree with me. Well, math didn't agree with me. I thought I was good in math until I got to college. So, then I went to the graphic arts." To graduate with a teaching certificate, she needed a fifth year of college but she wanted to graduate. "I was ready to graduate", she said, "so I did basic art to just get out."

After college, she tried working as a substitute teacher and found that, despite her earlier misgivings, she wanted to teach. She returned to college to earn a teaching certificate. During that time, she met and married her husband. He was already in a master's program in a seminary in New Jersey, so she decided to join him before finishing her teaching credentials and left Alabama for the North.

When she arrived in New Jersey, she worked as a substitute teacher in Rivertown, a nearby inner city school district for a few months until the director of the pre-school for the children of the seminarians offered her a job. She enjoyed teaching preschool, but wanted a family. After two and a half years, she became pregnant. She stayed home with her daughter, London, for three years until the fall of this school year when she decided that she wanted to go back to work. Through her a connection at her husband's church, she gained the instructional assistant job.

The basic skills math teacher at Water Stream School was her connection. "Mandy Whiterock. She goes to our church. And she knew that I was looking for a job and she gave me everybody's name to contact. And everybody seems to like me." Despite her positive impressions, she was worried about the nature of the assignment, as a one-to-one with a child with a behavioral problem. "Cause I thought, I don't want to be around a child that likes to fight. Then I would have to restrain all the time. But I don't think that would be the problem with her [Jewel Daniels, the student to whom she is assigned], at least not with me. Cause in the other district that I worked with there were a lot of kids fighting. I did not want to deal with that. So this is a great change to be here." She paused for a few moments and remembered the fighting she saw when she taught in the South. "Even in Mobile, in the school I taught in Mobile." Water Wheel does not have fighting in the halls and she wonders: "I don't know if it's the whole district, or just this school." I assured her that all the schools in the district are generally peaceful and ordered. She went on: "Mandy told me all about the school district and 'You would like it', and I said 'OK.' "

Like Pat, she feels that she entered the job with ease. Her sponsor, Mandy, works in her school, and she continues her social association with her by having lunch with her daily. Other parallels with Pat existed: Tiffany plans to work in the future as a teacher. In her story about herself, being a paraeducator was a way station in her life. Like Pat, she notes that she does not have a teaching certificate, but has plans to get one.

Tiffany has a college degree, school teaching experience, a sponsor, a husband and a child. In addition, she completed course work toward her teaching certificate. All of these factors seem to increase her social status within the community of practice.

Her evident warm personality may have made her a desirable candidate for the job, because the child who Tiffany was hired to support, Jewel, has attachment issues. Like Tiffany and Mandy, Jewel is African American. I privately wonder if Jewel would more easily attach to Tiffany due this shared part of their identity, but Tiffany never alludes to or mentions race.

Tiffany in the Classroom

At 1:45 on February 13th, 2008, I walk into Cindy Sharp's fifth grade classroom. Books are piled helter-skelter, and there is an empty aquarium on the floor under a kidney shaped table. The walls seem bare compared to many other rooms. There is a picture of the Mona Lisa on the wall, and a stylized Japanese print that says "Hokusai".

The children are sharing five large microscopes. Tiffany, smiling and pretty in a Valentine's red sweater, sits at a table in the far right hand corner of the room, cutting onions on a small cutting board. She smears a glass slide with the onion with one hand and gives it to a waiting child while holding her nose with the other. Cindy tells her she is a "feasible scientist", a tacit verbal support for her continued work with the onions and acknowledgement that Tiffany is a member of the class. I count twenty-five children in the classroom, gathered in clusters by each microscope. They are talking to each other, but the room is not loud. A pleasant hum of voices prevails. The students seem purposeful and I think I am looking at future medical researchers.

Cindy announces: "Jordan is not the boss, but he is the expert, because he did this in his other school." Jordan evidently transferred from another school earlier in the year. Cindy then rings a small bell and says loudly: "Please do not make me ding again. You are going to have to listen to your professor when you go to Harvard. Use the low power lens, not the medium or the high." Tiffany continues to smear slides and talk to a few children. While Cindy directs the entire class, Tiffany works with a small group.

Chapter 6: Tiffany Washington For Now

Tiffany has one of the simplest schedules of any of the paraeducators in the study. She is with one teacher, all day, with two exceptions: lunch duty, when no teachers are present, and the daily special, such as music or foreign language. Her student, Jewel, set several fires in the school last year. Tiffany has a dual purpose: the administration would like Jewel closely supervised to prevent another fire while her child study team case manager would like to see Jewel bond with an adult.

While the children immerse themselves in their scientific observations, Cindy comes over to me with an essay that Jewel wrote. Despite my explanation for my presence in her class, and the fact that I am not officially assigned to Jewel as her case manager, Cindy wants to share this work. I read it over, while trying to keep an eye on Tiffany. As during my observation of Pat, the teacher sees me in my usual role. I hear Tiffany's soft southern lilt as she talks to Meyata. Meyata is tall for her age and is dressed in tight jeans and tee shirt, with dangly earrings. At eleven, she looks fourteen.

While I read Jewel's essay on the upcoming presidential election, Tiffany cooks a bag of popcorn in the microwave oven in the back of the classroom. She gets the bag out of the oven and walks over to Meyata's group, to look into the eyepiece of their microscope. Meyata puts her hands on her hips and says: "Andrew, you are not the boss of the microscope." Tiffany chats with Andrew quietly and he smiles. The students stop arguing. Tiffany solves the problem between the two students quietly and unobtrusively through conversation.

Tiffany moves back to her corner and the kidney shaped table to clean up the onions and to dispense small handfuls of popcorn. Cindy announces that the science work is done and that the children need to hand in their lab reports because they are moving to independent reading and writing. As the children bring their cleaned and dried slides to Cindy, she hands them to Tiffany without a word. They seem to know what to expect from each other in their daily routine without talking, which is evidence of their mutual membership in a community of practice.[109] Tiffany inspects each one and nods as she puts them away in a cardboard box. "Shakespeare Club in the hallway!" Cindy says. Over half the children take books and leave the classroom for the hallway and Cindy follows them, saying as she leaves the room: "No talking, resist the urge!"

Tiffany is left in the class with eleven students. Jewel tells Tiffany that she hurt her tooth at lunch. Tiffany looks at the tooth and then tells her: "No nurse. Read." Jewel replies: "I don't have a book" and Tiffany rejoins: "Get a book." Another child asks her a question, which she answers and then turns to watch Jewel, who now wanders around the edge of the classroom. "Jewel," she calls "get your thing." Jewel says: "Oh, yah," in acknowledgement, gets her book, settles into her seat and opens it.

Jordan now tries to get Tiffany's attention. Tiffany graded his social studies test. He wants her to change his grade, he tells her. He has misspelled the name of the state of Ohio and he would like her to see his cursive "a" read as an "o". He smiles as he argues and both he and Tiffany are pleasant with each other. "I need to get an A", he says. He eventually gives up and walks away. Tiffany does not change his grade. She knows the procedures in this community of practice and her role within it as a giver of grades and authority figure.

Tiffany then moves around the room, picking up bits and pieces of equipment from the recently completed lab. Alfred brings

---

[109] Wenger, 1999.

her a pair of tweezers and she says: "I just put them away." He smiles and says: "I'm sorry." She replies: "No problem."

She turns to Jacob and asks him to empty a pitcher of water into the classroom sink, and he makes a pun: "I can't, I'm drawing a picture". She gives him a look and he laughs and takes the pitcher and empties it into the sink. Unlike Pat, Tiffany seems to have her own source of authority and does not reference the teacher constantly. The two participants demonstrate the range of possible ways to fulfill this role.[110]

Now, she scans the classroom observing the students, comparing their behavior to what she knows they should be doing in this community of practice. She tells one child: "Read. Get a book out." As she walks to her table, she sees that Jewel is not sitting at her own desk, but has slid into Tiffany's. Tiffany says to her: "If you don't mind could you get off my seat?" and Jewel leaves, seeming happy to have drawn Tiffany's attention. Tiffany and the students both know the guidelines for acceptable behavior, another sign of a community of practice.[111] Tiffany observes, makes a social judgment about the behavior she sees, communicates to students who she decides should change their behavior and expects them to adapt to her expectations. Tiffany shows that she has authority based upon expectations the teacher has set up.

Students come into the classroom from the hall, put their books away and grab instrument cases. Cindy enters behind them and urges them to get to band on time. Tiffany says something to one of the returning children about giving her the Macbeth books and the child responds: "Don't say that word. There is a curse on it!" Tiffany responds with "What?" to the child who is quickly leaving

---

[110] Connell, 2002.
[111] Wenger, 1999.

the class with his instrument in hand. I talk to her about "the Scottish play." She says: "They must have heard that outside", meaning that the children must have just had a lesson mentioning the curse out in the hall with Cindy while she was in the classroom. She goes to a student's desk, where he has left a two-page handout from the Shakespeare Club. Tiffany sits at her table and reads Cindy's handout on the history of the play. While she tries to concentrate, Jacob leaves his desk and stands in front of her flashing an engaging smile. "I'll show you my picture." And I realize that he is being ingratiating, in a fifth grade way. Tiffany smiles at him, shakes her head and points back to his seat, to which he retreats. The remaining children are working quietly and purposefully. Tiffany settles back to her seat to complete reading the handout on Macbeth, as I leave the classroom. Tiffany continues the process of her engagement in the classroom.

It is 10:35 a.m. on May 12, 2008. The students are taking a quiz when I enter the room. Tiffany sits in the back of the room, at the table she usually occupies, correcting math quizzes. Jewel is the first student to complete the assignment.

Jewel brings a book to Cindy first and then to Tiffany. Jewel glances at me and passes me by as she returns to her seat. I am clearly not part of the class in her mind, which serves as evidence that a community of practice exists.[112] Two boys chat with Tiffany and these are the same boys I have seen chatting with her during previous observations. A girl, Sara, comes to talk to Tiffany, and very quickly, Jewel moves to Tiffany from the other side of the room. Jewel tries to talk to Tiffany by drowning out Sara. Tiffany tells Jewel that she will only talk to her about her reading assignment. Jewel asks to sit with Tiffany but Tiffany says "No."

---

[112] Wenger, 1999.

Chapter 6: Tiffany Washington For Now

Jewel argues with her but Tiffany reiterates: "I'm sorry, but no."
Jewel looks sulky, but again, she does what Tiffany tells her. Sara
finally completes her sentence.

Jewel has more emotional needs and fewer functional methods
of getting them met than her fellow students. Tiffany curtails those
inappropriate behaviors when she observes them by instructing
Jewel in appropriate ways to secure attention. Tiffany shows that
she understands the underlying shared rules of this community of
practice: we are here for academic reasons primarily and must
politely share adult attention. She also shows how she has
interpreted her job, given vague guidelines. She decided that she is
not here to fulfill Jewel's emotional needs unless Jewel conforms
to classroom standards.

Cindy announces a quick play practice. She tells the students
that they each need to have a script and "If you don't have a script,
makes friends with someone who has a script." It is almost time for
lunch, which starts for them at 11:05. The public address system
crackles with the voice of the office secretary. She announces:
"The pizzas are here." Tiffany goes to the main office to get the
pizzas. Tiffany leaves the classroom without direction from Cindy,
showing her implicit understanding of the routine and illustrating
her membership in a community of practice.[113] While she is gone, I
find a script to read. The play is about the holocaust and
concentrates on the plight of some Jewish passengers trapped on a
ship.

Tiffany brings back three pizzas from the office and their
enticing smell wafts throughout the classroom. Cindy directs Alex
to read the script next, and Tiffany acts as the audience. Cindy tells
me that this is the story of the St. Louis and that less than one-third

---

[113] Wenger, 1999.

of the passengers survived the war. Within ten minutes, the script reading is over. Cindy tells the members of the Shakespeare Club to get out their copies of Hamlet. I am starting to understand that the Shakespeare club is a self-selected group of students who give up their lunch and other free time to read Shakespeare. Tiffany lines up the rest of the class to go to the cafeteria for lunch. Jewel takes this opportunity to rejoin: "I'm coming as fast as I can" and in response, Tiffany sends her to the end of the line. Jewel pushes her way to the front again, but Tiffany sees the ploy and redirects her to the back of the line.

Tiffany enforces routine, again showing she understands the underlying rules in this community of practice and her place of authority within it. Tiffany launches the long line down the corridors, through the central hall and around the back of the kitchen to a side entrance to the cafeteria. It will be inside recess, so Tom and Jerry cartoons are flickering across the big screen on stage and the sound track is at a deafening level.

Despite the noise, I hear Jewel say: "I need someone who likes me," in a bantering manner. Tiffany sits with her and three other girls from her class. Jewel seems less secure in her relationship with Tiffany than she seemed on previous observations. Later in the day, Tiffany tells me that just this morning she told Jewel that she plans to move back to Alabama at the end of the school year and she will not go to the middle school with her next year. Since Jewel was diagnosed with an attachment disorder, her discomfort with Tiffany leaving is understandable.

Tiffany's Process of Membership in the Classroom
Observe
Tiffany, like Pat, feels that the teacher owns the classroom, and was careful that at the beginning of the year, she respected that

ownership: "But me being the aide, I tell myself this is her class, and I'm here to help. I will ask her: 'Do you need help, do you need me to grade papers, blah, blah, this and that?' And I help her out, but still it is her class and she needs to be in control of that class. Especially with the other (specials) teachers, I don't want to make them upset, like, 'she's trying to take over my class'. So, that's the first thing. Be there to help." She accepts the premise that teacher preference dictates her behavior in the classroom as strongly as does her own ability. This idea forms part of the figured world in which she works.[114] To determine how to help, she observes the classroom, both to learn what is acceptable behavior and to reinforce acceptable behavior in the students.

Communicate

Tiffany explains her relationship with the teacher she works with and in so doing, gives evidence of the purposefulness of their conversations.[115] "Cindy loves when I have input. We're always on the same page on Jewel or any of the other students. 'Maybe we should try to do this and that?' And she'll go 'Okay.' I mention that I observed her exchanging glances with Cindy in the classroom when they wanted to signal each other, without telling the children. Tiffany feels that she and Cindy communicate just with a look across the classroom, explaining: "Well, we've been in a classroom with each other since September, that's almost six months. Cause it's the same stuff every day, every day. Kids do the same things every day. So we know what's going on and we look. You know, almost like if you give a child a look," she demonstrates a serious glare. "That child understands that look:

---

[114] Holland, et al 1998. Holland and Wenger's concepts overlap and reinforce each other. Holland's idea that concepts are concrete to people adds to Wenger's community of practice to describe social processes.

[115] Wenger, 1999.

'Ok, I'd better sit down.' So we make a look: she's starting this or they're doing that, because we know what's going on. Because we are with each other almost eight hours a day, every day, we are going to learn sign language from each other." Tiffany sees that "sign language" as an outgrowth of their working relationship. That 'sign language' is a marker of a community of practice.[116] But to know what Cindy wanted her to do in the classroom, she feels they need more than sign language. Tiffany says: "We talk. We talk a lot. I could see us becoming friends, regardless. Cause, in the morning, we'll talk about outside stuff. My husband, her boyfriend. Not just necessarily school stuff." She attributes their mutual understanding to frequent and lengthy discourse.

Through conversations, she bonds with students. "A lot of kids, they adopted me somehow. And the girls flock to me more than the boys. When we walk in the hallway, they all want to walk with me. And all the girls, all the American girls and especially the Indian girls, they are just all over me. Sometimes I have to tell them, 'Oh, I'm not eleven years old. I know I kid with you, but you talk about stuff I don't want to hear about. Like, not bad, but one of the girls said: 'Oh, your butt is big.' I don't want to hear that. 'Why are you talking like that?' If you want me to sit with you, I don't want to hear certain things. You can tell me if you like a little boy, I think that's cute. But other than that, I don't want to know." Unlike Pat, she evades the role of the teacher's policewoman, by ignoring what the students should not say and instructing the children on appropriate topics of conversation when they are within her hearing. She and Pat have the same issue, but differing solutions. She brings her identity to this community of practice. Her ability to assess appropriateness of actions and products signals both the

---

[116] Wenger, 1999.

existence of a community of practice and realities within that community mutually acknowledged by all the members.[117]

Applying those agreed upon realities required thoughtful social judgment and communication with students and teachers. Tiffany found herself wavering between nurturing and assessing students. "When I'm grading the papers, I want to say, 'He knew that.' But he didn't write that. This one boy, he wrote this word, he had a "t" in it. This one word, he was writing so fast, instead of crossing the "t", he put the mark like way down at the bottom of the paper and I know that's supposed to go up here and if I didn't know him, I'd say: 'What is that?' So I told him, I said: 'Well, I have to mark this wrong.' He said: 'Oh, but Miss Washington, you know I was supposed to put it up there.' I told him: 'Yes, but you rushed through your work and didn't check yourself. Double-check your work. You didn't do that.' So that's frustrating, trying to get them to take their time and really look at their work and what they are doing." Tiffany's frustration is the frustration of a teacher and her authority to grade is the authority of a teacher. Referencing enforcing a school wide rule, she recreates a typical conversation with a student about a cell phone, alternating between her own voice and an imitation of a child's voice: "'Miss Washington, look, I got a new phone.' I tell them: 'Good. Put it away so you don't get in trouble.' 'But look how pretty it is. I've got new songs.' 'Ok, but I can't hear your songs. Put it away. If I see it again, I have to take it. Put it away.' That's that big sister feel. They all want to share stuff and I don't want them to get in trouble." Echoing Pat's use of words, she describes the crosswinds of a dual loyalty to the rules of the community of practice and to the students.

She notes that the children want her attention. "They all want

---

[117] Wenger, 1999 and Holland et al, 1998.

to tell me information all day long. In the beginning, it was just
Jewel that would come to me all the time and tell me all her
personal business, about her mom, her daddy, everybody. Now,
other kids come." She moved to a more central position within the
community of practice, as evidenced by the students understanding
her role and what she could do for them.[118]

Tiffany felt that a *lack* of communication was sometimes a
problem. "They [the supervisor and the case manager] just said:
'Oh, you just need to walk with her and watch her and keep her on
track.' I think if maybe they gave me a list [of what to do] or if I
knew her background it would be better. Cause I didn't know she
was adopted until later on and I think that might have helped with
some of these attachment issues if I might have known that. So I
just didn't know enough about her in the beginning. I think if they
gave me her background or told me to go look at her background
or something that might have helped me a little bit." Tiffany
believed that she could have adapted her own behavior to fit
Jewel's needs, giving herself agency.

Commit

She built her relationship with the students deliberately
because, she said: "I am interested in their lives. In the beginning
of the year, they used to all bring their lunch and bring their Indian
food. I would say: 'What's that?' And they would say: 'Indian
food.' I'd say: 'I know it's Indian food, but what it is?' They'd say:
'I don't know.' 'What do you mean you don't know? You're
eating stuff and you don't even know what it is?' So I would make
them find out: 'Ok tomorrow, whatever you have you better know
what it is. Or I'm taking some of your minutes from recess.' So,
they were eating food and they didn't know what it was. So, they

---

[118] Wenger, 1999.

all found out what it was. And they saw that I was interested in that, and I knew things about their culture. So, that's how some of the Indian girls got attached to me."

"My American kids, I knew about music and stuff that they like, so that's how they got attached to me. I related to them with different stuff...outside of school. Outside of math and English." She built her relationships with the children the same way she built her relationship with Cindy Sharp, through a mixture of helping in the classroom and showing her interest in people's lives outside of the bounds of school. And she had this discourse with them deliberately to build relationships.

"And you know, I give them my attention. I'll be walking by a kid and I'll ..." She demonstrates by giving her own ear a pull. "I guess I am more like their big sister. And it's good and bad at times. They treat me like a big sister. I have to yell at them. [I tell them] 'I don't want to be that teacher that yells at you.' I guess they can see that I really do care about them and want to help them if they have a question. I come right away. I tell them that I help them the best way that I can." Unlike Pat, she envisions herself as an authority in her own right.

Tiffany reports that she likes being with the children: "The whole class, I love all those little kids." She looks at her future anticipated identity. "And I treat them all like—well I think, that's how London [her daughter] is going to be. If I have a son, that's how he's going to be, right there, even when they act bad, and I try to discipline them. I laugh but I try not to let them see me laugh, that I can't believe they did that."

"I work with every single child in that class. So, I work with twenty-four kids in the class. And in the hallways, countless numbers. I kind of blurred the line a little bit between teacher and friend. Cause that's just how I am with the kids, so when I really have to step in and put my foot down and get serious: 'go over there for a little bit.'" She is very clear about the traditional relationship between teacher and student, and that she sometimes changes the boundary between the two. This understanding of roles again signifies the existence of a community of practice.[119]

Tiffany instructs her charge in acceptable social behavior and coaches and encourages the all the children to exhibit desired behavior. Two boys seemed to particularly enjoy her company, and sit by her work area. When I ask about them, she says: "They're close to me. It's funny, cause every time we change the room around, they always get to sit right there, next to me. I'll go: 'How did you get next to me? Didn't I put you over there?' Yeah, those two, Ahmed and Benjamin. Those are ones who come up to me and go 'bother, bother, bother.' I call them my sons. Those two little boys are like my sons and I just love them. They get on my nerves just like I imagine my son will get on my nerves. They need a lot of attention." She draws parallel between the students and her sons yet to be conceived. She adapts the role through the framework of the role of parent, a role she knows well.

She models the behavior she wants to instill in the students with gentle and consistent good nature. Her acceptance of the children is evident over the course of the months of observation and interviews. Her discretion is also evident. She does not tell tales about the children out of class. She is careful with me to give instances, and first names only.

Adapt

Tiffany and Cindy have an understood procedure in place for her to adapt to circumstances. "If it's Jewel, I'll jump in and say: 'Blah, blah blah whatever.' If it's some other kids and Cindy sees

---

[119] Ibid.

it, and I see that she is going to handle it, she'll say something and I may add my two cents. But other than that, I try to let her handle the other kids first. But if she doesn't see that particular child with whatever's going on, then I will say something, and then she will put her two cents in." Tiffany looks to Cindy as the lead teacher, but acts like an authority figure with the children when she follows this process.

"The other teachers, since I'm not as close to them, I don't say: 'Maybe we should do that.' But I tell them: 'If you want me to discipline her, I will step in.' But I try not to discipline her. I try not to step in too much." Tiffany looks at the teacher as the arbiter of her role with the student. Her relationship with the teachers is intertwined with the amount of time she spends with each one.

Tiffany considers what her possible future role with Jewel would be like if she were not moving back to her home state of Alabama. Jewel will be going to sixth grade in the middle school the following year. When I wonder if she would move up a grade to go with Jewel, she replies: "I don't know. To be honest, it's going to be something totally different because you are not going to be in the same classroom with the same teachers. Three or four different teachers you have to work with and it's not the same twenty-five kids."

"They might eat her alive if she has a grownup following her around. Like the kids, they ask me, 'Why are you here? Why do you follow her?' And to try not to embarrass her, I say: 'She needs a bodyguard. I'm her bodyguard.' Just saying old stuff like that. And so, they won't accept that in sixth grade. The kids will be horrible." She builds an anticipated future through self-discourse,[120] just as she anticipated her future children. Only this

[120] Sfard and Prusak, 2005.

case, she describes a possible future that she wants to avoid.

She understands the boundaries between teacher and student and between teacher and paraeducator. She works to develop relationships with both the teacher and the students, and infuses that work with a sense of fun. She articulates the difficulty of befriending the children when she sometimes must judge them to give them grades. Her position differs from Pat's. She adapts to the particular community of practice in which she works. Throughout the course of the study, she flexibly and pleasantly did what she could within her given circumstances. Although she emphasized communication as important, what she was communicating and the boundaries of that communication were confined to the community of practice.

Partner

She likes working with Cindy, because they have fun together. "She's silly, goofy and that's how I am. We're at the pep rally and we were in there dancing. We were the only two teachers in there dancing. The other teachers were sitting against the wall. We drove our kids crazy. 'No, you're embarrassing us.' 'Stop.' We said: 'No, we're having fun.' She's goofy. I don't know if you saw her today? With the little hat. A note on her hat that said two-thirds. For Two-thirds Day."

The class was studying fractions, and Cindy had declared that this was a day dedicated to the fraction "two-thirds". "She's goofy and she's fine. She's not crazy. She just tries to have fun and enjoy life. You'll find yourself laughing at her and with her at the same time. That's me and that's Cindy. She's weird and she's silly and she knows she's weird and crazy like that. I like that. She's fun, she's not some stuck up person."

She explains further: "I mean, I was not going to make a hat [with a logo of the fraction two thirds] and walk around there (outside the classroom). I might have made one in the classroom, but I wasn't going to wear it out. I am like that, but to a point, where I stop here and she'll keep going." Tiffany feels that she could have made a silly hat, but she would have stayed in the classroom, their community of practice rather than "out". This sense of belonging they mutually built is also a trait of a community of practice.[121] Like Pat, she feels that her relationship with the teacher is based upon something they developed beyond discussions of their shared work. Discourse with the teacher creates a social bond. Wenger suggests that this type of discussion is one aspect of a community of practice.[122]

They did talk about their shared duties and they worked out their roles for discipline within the classroom early in the year. Tiffany said: "And in the beginning, Cindy said: 'Let me be the dragon lady. I'll be the one. I'll fuss at them and stuff. You don't have to do that unless you want to.' And I said: 'I don't want to unless I really, really, have to.' She said, 'I don't mind.' I said: 'Good.'"

Initially, not all the children accepted her role in the classroom. She recalls: "In the beginning of the year, some of the kids just had no respect for me. They said: 'You're not a real teacher. I don't have to do what you say.' That hindered and it made me not even like the child sometimes. I talked to Miss Sharp and Miss Sharp had talked to some of the parents of about two kids. And a couple of times, Miss Sharp said like: 'She is a teacher, you have to listen to her.' That worked."

Like Pat, her authority comes from the teacher, but unlike Pat, she sees herself as a kind of teacher. Tiffany sees her role as an assistant teacher, who also serves as a tutor for an individual or a

---

[121] Wenger, 1999.
[122] Ibid.

group, saying: "I never get up in front of the class, presenting a lecture. Miss Sharp may say something, and I may add on to something she may say. But it's more a tutor than a teacher. Than actually teaching a whole group." She derives the boundaries to her authority and the understanding of her role through a deliberate division of tasks arranged with the teacher.

Summary

While Pat sees herself as subordinate to the teachers with whom she works because she is in a position with less authority, Tiffany sees herself in a narrower role than the classroom teacher, not because of lack of authority, but because of lack of responsibility for the entire classroom. She implies, however, that she sometimes has a sense of being in-between the students when she talked about being "a big sister", just as Pat does. Like Pat, she has a sponsor into the school district. Having a college degree, a husband and child, add to her identity.

Although she does not look at working in this job or living in this geographical area as her ultimate destination in life, she seemed content with her current situation. Like Pat, she views herself in a way that is complex and fits into her perception of the other people in her community of practice, echoing Reich's assertion that identity is multifaceted.[123]

Tiffany taught in a private nursery school, and attributes her ability to work in the role of paraeducator to both that experience and her college work. She feels she was prepared for the job. She only needed to set up the parameters of her role within the classroom with the teacher Cindy. The evidence is abundant that Tiffany is working within a community of practice. For example,

---

[123] Reich. 1991.

Chapter 6: Tiffany Washington For Now

Tiffany and Cindy use facial signals to communicate, that was exclusive to them, but which Tiffany describes as "signing". This ease of communication in a method known to the insiders in a community of practice is another example of being an insider.[124]

The observations both confirm the existence of a community of practice and Tiffany's membership in that community. Tiffany has advantages over Pat in creating her place within the classroom. She is only in one classroom for seventy-five percent of the school day. Like Pat, she also seems to have a good match with her teacher: both have a pronounced sense of humor. Her references to the increased respect and friendliness that the children display toward her since the beginning of the school year marks the movement that she made in moving from an outsider to an insider position.

With a good personality match with the teacher in the classroom and time to nurture a working relationship, Tiffany performs a role within the classroom that she defines as a type of teacher. Her teacher treats her as a colleague and she spends most of her work time with her teacher. Tiffany, like Pat, creates and sustains her niche in the classroom through communication.[125] Many discussions center upon the work in the community of practice, such as how Tiffany expected Jewel to behave and what work the children should accomplish in class. She and the children resolved the ambiguities in their relationship through talking to each other. In addition, Tiffany deliberately discussed topics in their lives outside of school to create social bonds.

Ellen, the participant with the most formal training, also has a story to tell.

---

[124] Wenger, 1999.
[125] Juzwik, 2006;Erikson,1968

Chapter Seven
Ellen Montera
Outside, Looking Back

Ellen's Story of Self-identification

In the beginning of our first interview, Ellen lets me know that she has a New Jersey teaching certificate and a master's degree in education. She works as a paraeducator because wants to be a teacher in the district. She lives in the district and has three children attending district schools. She talks about her three children, ages fourteen, twelve and nine: "The youngest is in Centerville, the middle child is in Gardner and the oldest is in South High. All three different schools." Each school runs on a different schedule, and all are in East Brighton rather than Fieldtown where Water Wheel is located. Both the start and the end of her day require a great deal of coordination. Presently, her husband is self-employed and works from home right now due to a downsizing of his previous employer, which makes her schedule easier. She mentions that he emigrated from Argentina. While part of Ellen's background is Hispanic, her accent is decidedly from the Bronx.

Ellen continued her story: "I do have four years teaching experience back in New York. I worked in East Harlem and in the Bronx. Then we moved to New Jersey and I stayed home with my children for eight years. So I recently returned to work about two years ago. Unfortunately, returning to teaching has been more challenging than I expected. So, that is why I am an instructional assistant."

Chapter 7: Ellen Montera Outside, Looking Back

She explained how she became a teacher. "I made my decision to go into teaching when I was around sixteen. I went to the Appalachian Mountains with the school I was in, with a group of nuns and a group of students. We worked a lot with the children academically and also with different arts and things while we were down there. And it was there that I decided that I wanted to go into teaching. I felt a calling. I felt the calling to be a teacher."

Ellen's vocational and educational odyssey started in the Bronx where she grew up and attended high school. After high school she went to college for two years. "I ran out of money. I took a year, well a year and a half from school and worked in the diamond district. Actually learned how to grade diamonds while I was there." She went back to college, staying in the city and worked her way through her final years of school by working part time in the diamond industry.

She did her student teaching in New York City. She explained: "At City College, we actually did two semesters of student teaching. So I was in a fourth grade class and a K-1 class, in two different schools and two different very different atmospheres. One was a traditional setting and one was a very open classroom where they called the teacher by her first name. Which in a lot of respects is probably similar to how we do it here. They did small group work and different things. Everybody was on a different level but a very casual type of atmosphere."

Ellen stayed in New York for her first teaching position. "I was in a very poor school system when I was teaching in New York. I was teaching in East Harlem, it is considered Spanish Harlem, but of course, there is a mix [of ethnic groups]. It is very different, very little parent support. Unfortunately, a lot of children have parents that were in prison. Some were being raised by grandparents. We were constantly looking for abuse. Materials were very scarce, sparse. Teachers had to supply a lot of their own materials. Not a lot of administrative support. Basically you are on your own or you can find a couple of teachers that can be a support. Not a lot of community support. And technology was very different. Children walked to school. They weren't bused to school so we always saw the caregiver with the child. So a lot of times the parents would stop me and ask me something on a daily basis. I didn't even have a computer in my classroom and the only time the children were exposed to computers was when they went to computer class, which was worked into their specials during the week. I basically communicated with parents through the mail. They would write a letter and I would respond by mail or in person. I think we had more interaction with parents and grandparents than maybe some teachers have in this school. It was very different from here."

She continues her story: "And then I graduated and actually had my child shortly after that. But I worked with him and my mom helped me with him and then I had my second one and I was still working. But then, right after that we decided to move to New Jersey and we left my mother. And I really didn't want to put my kids in childcare at that time. And then we decided to have another child. So, especially with three of them at home, it just seemed to be the logical thing for me to stay at home. I stayed home with them for a number of years, so when my youngest daughter started first grade, that's when I returned to work. I was just waiting for her to be in all day school when I went back to work. It worked out."

Ellen puts her family needs before her work needs. She implies in her discussion, that she has a choice to stay home. When she decided to come back into the work world, she was able to search for employment on her terms that met her needs and her family's needs. With her husband usually working in New York, she needs to get the children on and off the school bus. She confines her working day to school hours and the district school calendar so she sees her children off to school and greets them when they come home. To her, working in the district is the only feasible option.

She has no connection to people in the schools, unlike Pat and Tiffany. "Actually, even being officially hired as an instructional assistant wasn't that straight forward. I had to start out as a substitute. I took a lot of long-term instructional assistant positions because my children are so relatively young. I like knowing where I am going to be every day. I didn't know if I did a substitute [job] where I was going to be, so when they had instructional assistant positions available for two weeks at a time or two months at a time, I took those. So I started off as a two-weeks, then a one-month instructional assistant. I would still be considered as a substitute [without the benefits of a full time employee] and then they just kept adding on months. Before I knew it, I was there for the remainder of the year. Then the following year, I still didn't receive a teaching position so I continued as a substitute. And once again, I found myself doing basically the same thing: taking a long-term instructional assistant position. I found myself working one-on-one with a child. Then I realized that I needed to go to the next step so I spoke to them (the principal and the special education case manager) about getting hired as an instructional assistant. Last January I became hired as an instructional assistant at French Town School. And then this year they transferred me over to Waterwheel."

Her experience at French Town School was varied. "I'd done two different things over there. I worked one-to-one where I was in one classroom [with one student] all day and that was relatively easy. I just followed him to different activities. But when I went from class to class, that was a lot of running around. But then I'm doing a lot of running around this year. A lot." This year, the principal gave Ellen a schedule that has her in more different classrooms in the course of the day than any other paraeducator on staff. She ended up with the left-over over bits and pieces due to several factors: as a late transfer from another school building her capacity and talent is unknown, and secondly, she is not hired to work with a particular child but to work with many children who need help in many general education classes for science and social studies.

In addition, she has no sponsor to help her with entry into the district. No one knows her in the school because while her children are in the district, they go to schools in schools in East Brighton, rather than Fieldtown, the location of Water Wheel School. Her story did have some convergence with Pat's and Tiffany's, but in a way that confirms their understanding of what is important to entry into the community of practice. In the absence of what they considered to be important, Ellen reports difficulty in gaining entry to the community of practice. Ellen is restless in this particular role in the school.

"I feel the need to move to the next step to become a teacher again. Especially, it is hard when you were a teacher and you are not a teacher any longer. I miss it. I miss being able to have my own class and work with them all day long. It's hard, especially when I am out for recess. You feel like you are not reaching your potential. Some days. I try not to look at it that way all the time, but there are certainly times when that crosses my mind. My own children still need a lot from me. But at the same token, I guess I want to have my cake and eat it too."

Like Pat and Tiffany, having a college degree signified an important achievement in her life story. She also mentioned that she did work in the past as a teacher and planned to work in the future as a teacher. She noted that this is not her first year as a paraeducator but it is her first year in this school building. Like Tiffany, to Ellen having a husband and children also seemed to be an important part of how she sees herself and a source of pride. She did not have a sponsor, but she did live in the district. Her story contained references to changes of plans. Like Tiffany and Pat, working as a paraeducator is not her career goal, but an occupation that serves a purpose for the present.

Ellen in the Classroom

8:50 am on May 9th, a rainy Friday, and children fill the halls, streaming to their first period classes. I see Ellen walking in the hallway with Melia. Waves of children are washing against them both, like rocks in a stream, because they walk slowly. Melia is only staying on her feet because Ellen is grabbing her shirt from the back. Melia's long pants hide the leg braces, but she walks with a stiff legged gait. Braces on her arms are more noticeable. Melia has a degenerative muscle disease that makes her progressively weaker. Her long braid swings as she walks awkwardly into Leslie Stands fourth grade Learning and Language Disabilities class. "LLD" is the shorthand name for this self-contained class, where the students spend most of their school day.

There are three other children in the classroom. Nicole is a pale, slight girl who stutters and does not read well. Drew is a recent transfer student with a moderate reading problem, who seems out of place with his earring and short bleached locks. Ahmed is here because his parents insisted that he needed the academic challenge despite his poor capacity for academic work. He looks confused much of the time I observe him. Ellen is assigned to this classroom as an instructional assistant for this one forty-minute period, every morning. Another assistant, Mothi Rayam is in the class as well but she is assigned for the entire morning.

Ellen helps Melia into her seat, where Melia lands heavily, with legs outthrust. Ellen then turns to me and lets me know that this class will be social studies. I look around the classroom in the few moments before the teacher is ready to start instruction. Five student desks and chairs are clustered at the front of the room by the white board. Four are arranged in a semicircle, with the fifth desk and chair facing the four. An additional chair is placed between two of the student desks, but that chair is not for her, it is for Mothi. There is a spare student chair against the wall, which Ellen relocates to a position between Melia and Nicole.

Leslie now moves from her teacher's desk, carrying her social studies textbook and comes to the student's desk facing the semicircle of students. She opens the book and announces that they will be reviewing the events that led up to the American Revolution. Each child is asked to open their textbook to page twenty-nine. With Ellen and Mothi's help, the four do so. Leslie begins to review "The Declaration of Independence" by telling the children about the contents of the document through the metaphor of the king as a parent.

Ellen points to the textbook page to direct Melia's attention. Leslie shows a copy of the Declaration of Independence and points to John Hancock's signature. Ellen turns the page of the textbook for Melia who sits with her hands folded and her feet crossed. Leslie reads a few lines from the Declaration of Independence.

As Leslie is talking, the physical therapist enters the room quietly and mouths "sorry" as she takes Melia for her therapy session. Ellen demonstrates her understanding of her place in the hierarchy—physical therapy trumps support by a paraeducator- by closing Melia's textbook and placing it in her desk. As Melia leaves the classroom, Ellen turns to Nicole and points to the page in the text. She has shifted her posture so that now she is bending to the right, over Nicole's desk. She becomes engaged, without the child or the teacher requesting the help. I am not sure this is a sign of her membership in a community of practice because Nicole did not need the help when Melia was in the room. Drew seems to understand what Leslie is saying. Ahmed is staring at the ceiling lights, but Mothi is trying to redirect his attention. Leslie points out signatures, saying: "That's why Betsy Ross got to make the flag, because her first husband's uncle signed." Ellen turns to Mothi and says: "I have to go." Ellen's work in this classroom is dependent upon her schedule. She must leave the classroom in the middle of instruction to get to her next assignment. Nicole returns to working on her own.

Ellen is out the door and heading to the other side of the building, trying to dodge the between-class traffic in the halls. For an elementary school, there is a lot of movement between classes and thus the wide hallways are clogged with students and teachers, especially at the intersection where all three main hallways of the building converge.

. At 9:35, inside Rick's class, the children are starting to take a social studies test. I know that Rita Subbu, a paraeducator, works in this class as a one-to-one with Karl Wundt, but I did not know that there is a third instructional assistant here as well. Galita Shah is an instructional assistant assigned to classes with children who qualify for free and reduced lunch, under a state program. She is also in Rick's room this period. In addition, two juniors from nearby Walker University are observing the classroom.

With the addition of Ellen and myself, the room feels crowded with people, furniture and belongings. The test the children are taking is an open note exam and the teacher is answering student questions about the process. Without greeting the teacher, Ellen starts helping a student. This lack of greeting is a sign of membership in a community of practice.[126] A second student asks her to go over his notes, which she does. The classroom has one wall made of a hanging plastic partition that can be folded back to open to the neighboring classroom. The room dividers are partially open and Rick is conferring with Rae Pound, the teacher he partners with for social studies and science. He and Rae revisit the issue of which packets and notes the students can consult for their open book exam.

While he chats, I look around the classroom to see how Rick arranges the space to hold so many people. At the front of the classroom, Rick has his desk with his computer pushed into one corner. Four feet to the left of that desk, he has a tall red director's chair, with the white board behind him. Student desks face his chair and are clustered in groups of two's, three's and four's. Hooks for coats are on the left hand wall, and coats are both on those hooks and on the floor with book bags spilled at the base of the mound of coats. Some coats and book bags pour out into the space that is intended for an aisle alongside the desks. In the back of the class, arranged so that there is still enough room to pass through to the adjoining classroom, are five computers. The other walls are graced with posters on writing strategies, essays the children wrote, the cursive alphabet, a Philadelphia Phillies's baseball team banner, plus a poster exhorting "Let Learning Take You Around the World."

One of the students tells Ellen that he left his notes for the test at home and asks if he can have a copy of his friend's set. Ellen

---

[126] Wenger, 1999

leaves the classroom to go to the nearby teacher's workroom and make a photocopy of the two pages of notes. When she returns, Ellen lets Rick know that the child with the notes left at home belongs to Rae's class, so the three of them, Ellen, Rick and Rae, gather at the boundary of the two rooms and talk. They reach an agreement and Rae says: "Ok, no photo copies. Let's see how they do."

Ellen defers to the teachers, although from her actions, she is ready to give out the photocopies that she made. This social behavior demonstrates her understanding her place in the hierarchy and her adaptability. Rick starts to distribute the tests, but Ellen and Galita quickly take them from his hands and take over the task showing that they both know that this is something within their role description, another community of practice behavior.

Rick starts to give directions about the test to both classes. A few children ask questions and he clarifies his directions further. While the children take the test, Rick goes to his desk to do paperwork. One child, Kara, tells Rick that she found a mistake on the test and he sends her to tell Rae. Rae tells her to alert Ellen, which she does. Ellen is kept in the community of practice through the sharing of information.[127]

Another child, Lara, comes and confers with Ellen. Ellen is standing at the edge of the class, with her back to the wall. Galita is positioned the same way on the opposite side of the classroom. A third child asks Ellen a question. Karl starts talking in a loud, high-pitched voice, saying repeatedly: "I can't take it!" Ellen ignores Karl and Rita, the paraeducator assigned to him who immediately takes him out of the room. Ellen goes to a student who is raising his hand, while Rick remains at his desk, completing paperwork.

---

[127] Wenger, 1999.

Rick leaves the classroom at 10:08. A few minutes pass and Ellen lets Rae know that the children have almost completed the test. Rae looks up from her paperwork and tells the children "Give me up to three things you learned for extra points." The children write for a few more minutes and then Ellen collects the tests. Rick is still out, but Rae is taking care of both classes when Ellen leaves for her next assignment. This narrative illustrates the boundaries in authority between the teachers and Ellen: Ellen can bring information to the attention of a teacher and give advice, but the ultimate decision-making belongs to the teachers. She spends time tacking, moving sideways like a sailor pushing against the wind, between teacher and student, student and teacher, ultimately getting where she needs to go, but taking a lot of time to get there. She does show evidence of belonging, despite her deference, in the classroom. In the forty minutes she has spent in the class, she has demonstrated sustained mutual relationships with the teachers, the other paraeducators and the students, a sign of membership in this community of practice.[128]

Ellen walks just around the corner for her next assignment. The children are making pinwheels and eating muffins in the hallway. Ellen is now working with fifth graders, in contrast to the fourth graders she was working with during the earlier part of the morning. The teacher, Bonnie Schwartz, gives her a quick overview of what the class is doing now and will be doing for the next forty minutes. Ellen asks: "Are we working in the hall?" and Bonnie replies: "Yes." Ellen needs orientation, a sign that she is not a member of this community of practice.[129]

Bonnie is a tall, big boned woman whose deep voice carries well through the children's chatter when she announces: "Do the

---

[128] Wenger, 1999.
[129] Ibid.

May-June packet!" One of the students Ellen is assigned to assist, Mark Cole, says: "I don't have a May-June packet." Bonnie gets him one and suggests to Ellen that she take Mark to the library. The library is a good three minute walk away and I do not understand why Bonnie would want him so far away, unless she looks at Ellen's help as a respite for her class and herself. Mark overhears the conversation and says that he wants to do the packet here, with the other students. He sits down on the floor and starts right to work. Bonnie tells him: "Mark, Mrs. Montera is going to help you, because I know you want to be a good helper." Ellen does not insist that Mark go to the library, and after the initial remonstrance, neither does Bonnie. Ellen looks around and asks Bonnie: "Do these markers go in the classroom?" Ellen's question shows her lack of membership in this community of practice, because she does not know the insider information.[130] "No," Bonnie, replies, "they go on the tray." She points to a tray with scissors and materials on a small desk set against the wall. Ellen helps Mark work on the activity packet for about ten minutes until Bonnie says that it is time to clean up and come back into the classroom. Ellen helps Mark put away scissors and markers. Bonnie tells him: "Mark, you did a good job cleaning up" and directs the children back into the class. Ellen follows Mark, puts her belongings down on the floor and finds a spare chair that she pulls up beside him.

The students continue to work on the sheets in the packet at their desks. The papers contain social studies, science, math and reading work. Mark has a problem with the math work on one page. Ellen helps him through the first computation and then suggests that he talk to Burea, a student who has a good grasp of

---

[130] Ibid.

the math concept of subtracting decimals. Burea, however, seems to be having trouble with the same problem, so Ellen finds a math book, and turns to the appropriate chapter. She encourages Burea. Meantime, Mark has found part of a transparency from an overhead projector on the floor and is squinting at the lights on the ceiling through it. Bonnie tells him: "Mark, I'll take care of that." Mark tries to put it in his desk, but Bonnie sees what he is doing and says: "No. That was supposed to go in the trash." Ellen is still with Burea, who starts to sneeze repeatedly. By the time he gets a tissue and returns to his desk, Ellen is glancing at the clock. The relentless clock tells her to disrupt her work yet again and leave. She asks Burea to take her copy of the math book to the filing cabinet, while she gathers up her red cloth bag, purse and jacket to head out of the room and down the hallway.

Ellen says that she does not use the locker in the workroom to store her belongings, because it is too small. It is easier for her to carry everything from room to room throughout the day. She returns to Rick Johnson's fourth grade classroom. The students are reading historical fiction. When Ellen asks Rick what she can do to help him, Rick gives her the raw materials for a bulletin board as well as some photocopying he needs for next week. Now that the rain is stopped and the sun is out, the class will go outside for more recess. Rick and the students, as well as Rita, the paraeducator who works with Karl, leave for the playground. Ellen goes to the copier room, rather than joining the class. The afternoon recess is typically one in which the adults catch up with each other as well as watch the children and is seen as a moment to bond with each other. Ellen is not included, suggesting that she is not seen as a full member of this community of practice, the one where she spends most of her work time.

She copies and we chat. She tells me that she would like to have her own classroom next year. There is no job security in being a paraeducator, because there is no tenure. She does not get a say in where she is placed and if she returns as a paraeducator next year, she will not find out her assignment until two weeks before school starts. Despite the drawbacks of her current work and the availability of teaching positions in nearby school districts, she wants to stay in the East Brighton-Fieldtown district where her children attend school. Her husband likes her to be home for the children and she likes it, too. It is part of their culture, since he is from South America and she is, she says "half Columbian."

While Ellen has better formal credentials, she does not have the strongly accepted membership that Pat and Tiffany display. Even her lack of a place for her bag and coat signals a nomadic existence. She struggles to earn a space in the community, giving evidence to its existence but not to her membership. The observations exemplify her exclusion from many of the classes in which she works, providing a context for views she conveyed during interviews and informal discussions.

Ellen's Process of Membership in the Classroom
Observe

Ellen watches the behavior of the children and the teachers in the classroom to determine what she should do with them. "I go around and ask the students 'How are you doing?' and if they seem to be doing okay on their own, I rotate to another table. And then, if there is ever a slow time in the class and it looks as if the children don't need my help then I go to the teacher and ask if there is anything I can do. Sometimes he [the teacher, Rick] sends me for photocopying, other times it might be a particular child in the class who needs to catch up with some work and then I will go out in the hallway and work with them. When there is an actual lesson going on, I have more than enough work. Eighth period [the last period of the day] might be a little slow, because a lot of the children are out for instrument [lessons] or chorus. During those times, some children might catch up with work or I do some photocopying."

She feels that she tries to take cues from what she observes in the classroom. "If they are doing a science experiment, Mr. Johnson would run that and I would just be there as support and assist any groups that are having trouble with it. It really depends on the subject area and what else is going on. If there's a group of kids doing math problems, just a small group, I may go out in the hallway with them and work out there. And that would be more of an interactive role. It really depends on what the need is at a given time." She judges what is needed from what the children and the teacher tell her, not just from what she observes.

Communicate

It was no coincidence that Ellen thought about her job through the lens of her work in Rick Johnson's classroom. "I guess I enjoy working with Mr. Johnson the most. I am with him the most, I know him the most and I know the kids the most. We have our routine going. It's difficult when you are in a class on one period out of the week or two periods out of the week. It's hard to have too much of a relationship with anybody. You're just sort of a filler at that point." She is a visitor to those other communities of practice and shut out from membership by a lack of time spent within the classrooms. She feels that she has a relationship to Rick's class, a sign of a community of practice.[131]

---

[131] Wenger, 1999.

Chapter 7: Ellen Montera Outside, Looking Back

I ask her specifically about a problem I observed in Rick Johnson's class, with another paraeducator. Ellen thought that she was supposed to work with Alex, because he is a special education student. Galita Shah also thought she was supposed to work with Alex, because he is a Title I student. Title I is a government program to help students at risk for school problems. In fact, Galita and Ellen are both assigned to Alex because he is classified as eligible to receive both special services and Title I support. I had noticed Ellen speaking to Galita in the hallway after class about which children she is assigned to help.

Ellen clarifies: "In the retrospect, that was probably not the best location. I should have asked her to step to somewhere more private. I try to resolve things pretty quickly, because I don't like to have things linger. The teacher didn't really need to step in. She's an adult and I'm an adult. We should be able to resolve this on our own without having somebody else intervene. I ask her how she resolved the problem and she replies: "We never really discussed it after that one time. I noticed that a lot of times, she'll go out in the hall and work with students. She seems to like that separation." Conflicts arise, as they inevitably do, but Ellen has little time and literally no space in which to resolve them.

We talk about her piecemeal schedule. She is with five different teachers today. She sees "A lot of different teaching styles, but you know you just you work with everyone as best you can. I think it is hard for the teachers, too, like if I am only with them for one period, one time a week. It is hard for me to keep up with what the class is doing when you know I am not with them on a daily basis. But there are some teachers I am with every day and things go a little smoother when they know me and I know them."

Knowing each other is important in her becoming a member of the community of practice, and knowing each other takes time, she thinks. She feels that to know a teacher, she needs to work with him or her at least on a daily basis. We talk about her perceptions in the latter part of the school year, and she still feels that despite following her schedule for over six months, she has a hard time in rooms in which her appearance was less than one period per day.

Due to the fragmented nature of her workday, she carries a laminated copy of her schedule with her. "Believe it or not", she says, "I still refer to it. I have to get myself situated each day. It doesn't change that much, but a little bit from day to day. And then I do a couple of gym classes, two on Monday and two on Wednesday."

"When I need a substitute," she continues, "I try to get subs who know the children. Sometimes, the teachers give me a brief idea of what they are planning with the kids, but a lot of times I just jump in. Especially with Mr. Johnson, I am with his class every single day, so I know what material they are covering. Some of the other teachers, if I'm not with them very often, I just try to jump in." Jumping in was her phrase for trying to help the students without much direction from the teacher or sustained time in the classroom.

"Teachers really don't go into detail about what their lesson is going to be or anything. I just jump in. I don't really even know what is planned for that day, whether we are doing social studies or science. Sometimes I just have to listen to what they are saying to the class and follow along, because it changes from day to day. To a certain extent, the teachers treat IA's as colleagues. More so here than in the inner city schools. Here, it's more of a partnership." Despite her quantification of "more", she says: "They don't really consult or discuss with us. They just do that with their fellow teachers."

Chapter 7: Ellen Montera Outside, Looking Back

I ask her why the teachers did not discuss the day's lesson plans with her. She replied: "I think a lot of it is time is an issue. When you are coming in and the kids are already there, there is no time to discuss anything. Last year, the teacher that I worked with was a little more up front about when she had workshop, she'd say: 'I won't be in tomorrow morning.' But not all teachers are like that. But I was with her all day, too. It's a little different when you are with someone all day as opposed to just one, two or three periods a day." We have come back to the problem with her schedule again. Lack of time means lack of communication and she is less effective as a support for the children.

Commit

In addition to teaching and mothering, Ellen envisions herself in a protective role with her cognitively and physically handicapped students: "Sometimes the other kids say mean things to Burea and he can't protect himself. So, I need to explain to the children that they need to be more patient with him. And with Melia, from a physical standpoint, when we go into a crowded hallway, she holds on to me and I make sure that she is stable when we walk through the hallways. The kids just walk past you and bang into you, and the smallest little thing and she will fall over. I think I do take on a protective role."

She thinks that the children's reactions to her vary. "I would say that some children welcome me into their classroom. Welcome the help. And there's other children that make it clear that they do not want my help and would rather work independently. I think part of that is I am encouraging them to continue working and they don't want to do that. In fact, one student is even very clearly angry that I am with him. He'll actually come up to me and say, 'why must you follow me around? Why must you look at everything I do?' There are a couple of students who don't want our help. And unfortunately, they are the ones who need our help. I'm persistent. Eventually, they usually come around."

She makes a commitment in her work, even to the children with whom she has difficulty creating a working relationship. She elaborates on her relationship with students: "I am just always very respectful to them [the students] and try to be considerate of them. For instance, I know that Melia does not like to put her braces on in front of other kids, so I try to do it as discretely as possible, either in her classroom or in Mrs. Stands' classroom. Or a place that is not too populated, inside the bathroom when the other kids are not around. For the most part, it's the hand braces [I help her with].

"Sometimes, they tell me things in confidence, and I try to help them out with that. Like one time, Melia told me she didn't like to be on the exercise equipment outside in front of all the other kids with the physical therapist. She felt as if the other kids were looking at her. At that particular appointment, she was out during recess, so there were a large group of kids out there. I just relay the message, to let them know to try to do it at a time when it is less populated out there. I think that's basically the secret. I just try to make them feel as safe and as comfortable in their school environment as possible. I'm always honest with them and dependable, so I think that goes toward building trust."

Adapt

"I definitely feel a sense of accomplishment working with Melia." Ellen reports, "I feel that I am an asset to her and I try to make her have as normal of a day as possible so that she can still be with the other children. You know, in gym, there is really nothing that she is not able to do in gym. I'm just there to help her do all the activities that the other children do. Now, when it comes to bicycles, I'm not sure exactly what Miss Pourbois plans for that.

Maybe she'll have training wheels for Melia. She is always trying to adapt the program for Melia so she is never prevented from being involved with the rest of the class."

"In art, I think is a challenge for her and maybe for Burea as well. And I'm able to assist them in art as well. I feel a big sense of accomplishment. I'm like her right hand in some ways. She's able to go through her day." Ellen sees herself as an extension of the student, rather than an entity in her own right. As an extension, she does not do the adaptation but implements the adaptation done by teachers.

Partner

I ask Ellen if she sees her role of paraeducator any differently now than when she was a teacher. She casts back in her memory to her experiences with paraeducators when she was a teacher. "I know that when I was teaching and I had a paraeducator in the classroom, I couldn't even imagine life without her. In fact, my very first year of teaching, I had a k-one class. As a new teacher, it was overwhelming to begin with to have a K-1 [a combined kindergarten and first grade] class. So, a lot of times, I would have her work with the small group. She would do a mini lesson for kindergarteners, while I would teach the first graders. And now that I am an instructional assistant, I see that I could have actually even used her in other ways that I didn't. But I was a new teacher. You learn as you go along." Ellen feels that Rick Johnson, the teacher with whom she spent the most time during the school day, views her as an extension of himself. "I think that he thinks of me as another set of hands, basically," she says, rather than a separate entity. The day after our interview about her relationship with teachers, Ellen put a handwritten note in my mailbox that reads:

Mrs. Hull

I want to add to what was said yesterday. Even though I did say there is a certain "partnership", I believe it is limited. There is still an unwritten hierarchy. We follow the teacher's lead. We often keep quiet. We would never second-guess a teacher's decision or approach. That is why it is, was, difficult for me to approach that teacher the other day. It is simply not done.

I also believe when the teachers know about you, they treat you a little differently. When I was in another school, as an IA, more teachers knew my background and treated me a little more as an equal. For instance in the in-service [a training meeting held once each year for all the personnel in the district] many IA's [instructional assistants] were excluded from the conversation but when I jumped in, they [the teachers] were responsive and appeared to be interested in what I had to say.

Basically, as an IA you need to know your place. No matter what our educational background or previous profession, we will never be considered an equal such as a speech therapist, OT [occupational therapist], PT [physical therapist], etc.

I hope this clarifies a little. Sometimes, it is difficult to fully answer on the spot.

"Ellen"

In her letter, she notes that there are unspoken rules that govern her behavior. These unspoken rules are as real and concrete to her as the pillars that hold up the roof of the school, as part of her figured world.[132]

Summary

Ellen Montera is a highly trained former teacher who aspires to return to teaching. She views her current occupation of paraeducator as a method to gain entry to the East Brighton-Fieldtown school district. She sees the two occupations, teacher and paraeducator, as distinct and different. In fact, she feels she learned how to be a paraeducator through her experience of supervising a paraeducator when she was a teacher earlier in her career.

Ellen has the perspective of a former teacher. She talks about the contrasts between being a teacher and being a paraeducator: "I used to be more aware of the schedule during the course of the day and have the lessons planned and so on. A lot of times things don't always get communicated to us. If something comes up and we are supposed to be with a child, we are not always notified that that child is doing something else. Sometimes we have to seek that information on our own. There have been a couple of times that I've had to go looking for children because I wasn't told where they were. They were not where they were supposed to be."

Her ability to make decisions about her day is circumscribed by her sense of her place in the hierarchy, which is well below that of a teacher. In classrooms other than Rick Johnson's, she states she is a "filler" she says, more than a member. Unlike any other participant, Ellen carries her belongings from room to room. She has no space that belongs to her or to her belongings. Information is slow to flow to her. Many teachers use introductory preambles

---

[132] Holland, 1998.

prior to interactions. She lacks understanding of how to manage things in the other classrooms and did not share in any jargon or verbal shortcuts. Her missing connection to the classrooms proves her lack of membership in some classrooms and her circumscribed membership in Rick's classroom.

Ellen is clear that there are distinctions between the role of paraeducator and the role of teacher. "Being a paraeducator is definitely more personal. I think that some of the children confide in me [more] than they ever would with their homeroom teacher. Part of the reason is that I am with them during recess where they have the opportunity to open up to me, where in the classroom, you are focused on the subjects. You might not necessarily get into personal issues. And I definitely see the mothering come out, especially during lunch and recess. As the mother of three, I'm used to that." Like Pat and Tiffany, she uses the analogy of herself as a family member to describe her place in the general education classroom.

Despite wanting to be in a teaching position, Ellen values the advantages of less responsibility. "I have to say it's really nice not to have to worry about lesson plans. I think that's why a lot of us are happy being instructional assistants. You can plan to just go into work and not have to bring the work home with you. And have your weekends to yourself or to your children."

Ellen sees the ambiguity in her current occupation. "There are not a lot of things that are spelled out for us. Even a lot of our responsibilities are not spelled out. We just have to look to the teacher for guidance and see what is needed at that particular period. My education background, I mean, I know how to be in the classroom." She presumes that other paraeducators are experiencing the same need for directives from the teachers and that her experience as a paraeducator is the same as other paraeducators.

Ellen does not believe that she is lacking training or aptitude. She ascribes her difficulties during the day to lack of communication. "Maybe just to be a little more informed. It would be helpful. I think with instructional assistants, maybe our mailbox. I don't know about the other IAs [Instructional Assistants], but I know that I usually check my mailbox, because I don't have time during the day to check my email. And I don't even have access to emails, other than in the workrooms. To tell you the truth, I still haven't figured out how to use it. So, I usually just wait until I go home to check for emails. So, really, the mailbox is my only form of communication when I'm at school." The mailboxes, located in the main office, one for each staff member, are only used now to send hard copies of notices. Before email, people also used them to send messages during the day. With her schedule and lack of a home base, she has no way to check for electronic messages while she is at work.

Ellen is cut off from a major source of information in the school day, which may be part of why she feels ill informed on occasion. She lacks time for discourse with teachers and consequently, lacks membership in many of the classroom communities of practice to which she is assigned. Ellen does not have time to observe, communicate, commit to being a member of each classroom and adapt her behavior to each community and partner with each teacher. Lacking these behaviors, she cannot set up a positive feedback loop to help her learn in each setting. Ellen struggles to do her job, despite having the highest level of teacher training of all the participants. Her difficulty entering the community of practice suggests that time in the site is crucial to performing the job.

The Paraeducator: The Other Grown-Up In The Classroom

Brenda, the next participant, is not a novice like Pat, Tiffany and Ellen. She has the perspective of a seasoned veteran in the occupation of paraeducator.

Chapter Eight
Brenda Carlsen
Second to None

Brenda's Story of Self-identification

Brenda grew up in a small farming community in one of the midwestern prairie states. "When I was a kid, I always thought that I would be a doctor, a neurosurgeon." I could easily imagine Brenda in a white lab coat with a stethoscope slung around her neck. She would be decisive and reassuring. Her walk is solid and determined.

"Then when I grew up, I realized that I did not come from a wealthy family. We just didn't have the resources to support that ambition." Brenda approaches her story of her life with the declaration of what she did not become. She continues with what *did* happen. Thwarted at becoming a doctor, she decided to be a nurse: "I went to Methodist Hospital to apply to the nursing program and the woman said: 'You should really get your BSN [Bachelor of Science in Nursing] because that's the way it's going.' But the school I went to didn't have a BSN at the time.

I thought, maybe I'll go into education. I was a product of the early seventies coming out of school and at that point everyone was coming out with an education degree. It was very tough trying to get a job. So I did other things.

I worked as an assistant dietician at a major hospital in Peoria, Illinois. After a few years, I moved to a position in a small district hospital as an assistant dietician and assistant manager of the dietary department. I did that for five years." She nods and then continues her story.

"I wasn't going anywhere with that, so I went into a two-year post baccalaureate nuclear medicine program at St. Barnabas in Peoria, Illinois. I got my certificate in using radioactive materials as tracers you inject into patients for diagnostic purposes. When I graduated, I went to the Barnett Hospital in St. Louis, Missouri. I worked there two years, because that's about how long people last. You might get called out four or five times in your week of being on-call. You get home maybe at midnight and then you have to go back in at eight o'clock for your day shift. And then you had weekend call." She pauses for a moment to mark a change in her career path.

"I went to St. Matthew's where I was a senior technologist who trained the young people. And then I got interested in nuclear cardiology. I read and diagnosed EKGs, doing exercise studies with the patients. I worked in that field for ten or eleven years." Despite problems funding medical training, Brenda had a career in the medical field.

"Then I met my husband. He was doing his PhD at Rice. We married and he had a job at Penn, so we moved up here. And I worked at Penn in the vet school. I had my daughter but I was the administrative assistant for the associate dean for almost eight years. Then I got pregnant with the boys and we moved here. When the boys were born, I didn't work for about six years. I stayed home with them."

At fifty-eight years old, she is married and has three children: a daughter who is a senior in high school and twin ten-year old boys who attend fifth grade at the school where she works. She has a bachelor's degree in education, technical medical training and some graduate courses. She did not complete her master's program when "we got pregnant with the boys and they are twins". She further explains that she had a high-risk pregnancy, since she was forty-seven years old when she delivered them. Two circumstances influenced her decision to delay her workforce re-entry: one of the boys has mild special academic needs and her husband has a demanding but financially rewarding job. The job required long hours away from home but enabled him to support the family financially. Like Ellen, by not working outside the home, she could fill in the gaps in his parenting time.

"I did volunteer work in the schools and then realized that I needed to really get back in the job market. What can I do at home forever?" Brenda asks rhetorically, implying that there was nothing that she could do at home forever. "And by then my certification in nuclear medication was lapsed far enough that to really go back into it, I would probably have to pick up some courses again. So, I thought I would do substitute teaching and that way I could do what I wanted with my own schedule. I could work or not."

"Every once in a while I would pick up some IA (instructional assistant) jobs because that was what was available." She was assigned to work in Sharon Killigan's room. Sharon Killigan teaches a small, self-contained class of students with cognitive impairments in the borderline intelligence range or lower. "So, I was in Sharon's room and when she saw that I was ok with the kids, she said: 'What's your number?' We'll ask for you.'" Each substitute teacher is assigned a number to be used in an automated sub caller system. "So they'd asked for me a couple of times. And then Lee Ann took a pregnancy replacement." Lee Ann, a paraeducator assigned to Sharon's classroom, is a teacher who had taken the paraeducator position to get into the district in hope of getting hired as a teacher. Lee Ann took a temporary teaching position. "So, that position was open," Brenda continues. "Sharon said: 'would you like to work here? Are you interested in working with Tami?' Because Lee Ann had been Tami's one-on-one. And I said: 'Sure'. And being in medicine, I've always liked being around people and helping people."

So, that's when I started. Then I had Tami for about a year and a half. I had her all last year and about half of the year before." What she does not mention, because we both know it, is that Tami was notoriously difficult to work with and that Brenda worked with her very well.

When I ask her if it had been hard to become a paraeducator, she replied: "No, all I had to do was talk to Kate Spinnings. Sharon said: 'You have to talk to Kate.'" Kate is the supervisor of special education who hires paraeducators for work in grades preschool through fifth, which Pat mentioned in her entry story. And as things usually work in the school, probably Sharon spoke to Kate before she even mentioned employment to Brenda.

As with Pat and Tiffany, Kate Spinnings thought that Brenda was the right person at the right time for the individual student. Like Pat and Tiffany, Brenda feels that she entered the job with ease. Her sponsor, Sharon, is in her school, and they continued their association by working together daily for a year and a half. Having a college degree and further training is important to Brenda, but she bases her sense of competency upon experiences in the medical field. Although having a husband and children also seem to be an important part of how she sees herself, Brenda states that her competency comes from her training and experiences in the working world and not parenting. This job is where she is comfortable, despite other employment possibilities. She does not have plans to change nor does she have plans to become a teacher.

Chapter 8: Brenda Carlsen, Second To None

Brenda in the Classroom

Brenda is assigned to only one student, Martin, but he has a particularly complex schedule and he is a particularly complex child. At the beginning of the school year, he divided his day between four teachers. At the suggestion of Regina Thompson, his special education teacher for math, his case manager switched him from math class in Regina's room to another teacher's that was better suited to his level of math skill. Now, he is in his home room for three periods out of eight daily with Rachelle Delmonte, remaining in a resource room for two periods of reading and language arts with Regina Thompson, another resource room for one period of math with Shelly Plaistow daily, and with Florence Wang for science four periods per week. He is also with one or two other teachers one period per day for a computer class, foreign language, physical education, health, music or art. Brenda and her student work into five or six different communities of practice during one school day. Over the course of my observations and interviews, I observe how she adjusts her behavior within several communities.

First period, at 8:50 am on Friday morning, January 11th, 2008 and Rachelle Delmonte's students are scheduled for science instruction from Florence Wang, who is Rachelle's partner in what the staff calls a "double". Florence teaches science to her class and to Rachelle's, while Rachelle teaches social studies to her class and to Florence's. I open the door to Florence's room; I see a room full of children with purple plastic microscopes. This particular class is a hands-on lab, and each student has his or her own microscope at their desk. Twenty-four desks are divided into clusters of six, forming four contiguous flat surfaces. Children are moving purposefully from one table-like area to another, peering into microscopes, getting slides from each other, putting what looks like gray dust from vials on the slide surface, writing on a sheet from a stapled packet, talking, and laughing. There are two adults in the room. One is Susan Compton, a paraeducator who is assigned to several members of the class during three periods of the day, and the other is Brenda.

Brenda and Martin have a desk in one of the clumps of four. Martin has been diagnosed with a severe case of Attention Deficit/Hyperactivity disorder. He is prescribed daily medication that brings his activity down to a level that is sustainable in a classroom when he has a one-to-one assistant. He earned the assistant through disruptive behavior such as calling out in class, and flatly refusing to do work his previous two years of school. Brenda is at Martin's side, and only leaves his side once, briefly, during the entire period.

As Martin attempts to tap graphite on a slide, she offers: "May I suggest something?" After he prepares the slide, she reminds him to put the cap on the top of the tube of graphite, which he does. Martin looks through the microscope eyepiece and tells her that he has found an amoeba. Brenda takes a turn looking into the microscope and says: "This is interesting. What are the colors in there?" He does not answer her. He looks through the microscope again and says: "Green!" in a loud and exasperated voice. Brenda takes another turn at the microscope as well and says: "Green. Sure enough", in a calm and steady voice. Brenda then writes Martin's answer of "green" onto the lab report.

Once he decides what color the slide holds, he does not want to look at it again. Brenda tries to get him to elaborate on his answer of "green" with prompts such as: "sparkly, or clear?" but he gets up from his seat and walks away from her. She says: "Where are you going? We're not finished yet."

He comes back and looks into the microscope again and says: "It looks like a boulder inside it." Brenda tells him: "Draw what you are seeing." He stands by the desk to draw, bent over rather than sitting in his seat. After Brenda asks him about the color and the shape, she works down the list of characteristics of the samples, including the size and texture. She helps him complete the drawing, item by item, until the period ends.

She stays in the role, steady and unruffled, despite Martin's agitation. However much she may find him to be difficult, she pursues her social role. She uses her language, the tone of her language and her body language to assert her identity.[133] Brenda tells me later that I saw typical behavior because he has responds to directions and stays on task with great difficulty. She demonstrates a sustained relationship with Martin, evidence of membership in a community of practice.[134] Based upon that relationship, she asserts that she knows him better than anyone else and she can judge when he should or should not be held accountable. She states that she is professionally competent to decide when, where and how to make demands on Martin.

Now it is early February, and I am getting into the room where Brenda spends three periods of her day with Rachelle Delmonte, the general education teacher, and Susan Compton, the other instructional assistant assigned to the class. Brenda has told me that she feels that she is an integral part of this classroom. Rachelle is at the front of the class, Susan stands by the wall near the windows and Brenda is at the back, a few feet away from Martin. The students are writing essays and Martin is also working on an essay, but using his portable word processor, the AlphaSmart. He seems calmer here than in Florence Wang's class. Brenda looks at

---

[133] Fitch, 2003
[134] Wenger, 1999

Rachelle who nods towards the clock. Susan looks at Brenda, who nods. Brenda quietly talks to Martin, who leaves with her. Later, I find out that he needed to go to the nurse to get his Attention Deficit medication that his mother had forgotten to administer to him that morning. Rachelle wanted them to leave after Martin had finished a particular section of his work and while Susan would still be in the classroom, since she is only assigned to that class part time. The three adults were able to signal each other without exchanging a word, another sign of community of practice.[135]

February 25th at 12:40 p.m. and I am in Regina Thompson's resource room, where Brenda and Martin spend two periods of their day. In interviews, Brenda told me that she has the most difficulty working in this room. I am looking forward to observing how she navigates what she considers to be obstacles in this community of practice.

Regina's coat is tossed across a pile of papers behind her desk. A cardboard box full of books is precariously perched upon a chair. Every inch of the walls in this twelve by eighteen foot classroom is lined with full bookcases. In front of these bookcases are tables laden with a jumble of workbooks and piles of papers. Plastic bins, crammed with more materials, are under the tables. As a member of this school community, I know that the physical disarray is unusual.

In the scant remaining floor space, Martin and four other boys are seated in chairs behind student desks, while Brenda is seated in a chair without a desk. Regina finds a stool under a pile of papers for me to perch upon. With my entry, I have interrupted Martin who is explaining why he did not complete his homework. Brenda sits with her arms folded over her chest, while Regina listens with

---

[135] Wenger, 1999

both arms on her hips. Their body language says clearly to me that he is not pleading his case well. "The AlphaSmart was in the wrong place," he says. "And I didn't write. I had my first sleepover. I wasn't home for forty-eight hours." I am startled by the loud noise of Danny dumping a plastic bin full of pencils on the floor.

As Regina's attention moves from Martin to Danny, Brenda whispers to her "I'm going to have him do his homework." Now Gene starts to talk about his pants, which are checkered black and red: "He can't say anything about my pants!" I have obviously missed an earlier discussion. Regina ignores Gene's outburst and tells the students it is time to complete their journal entries. Danny starts to put the pencils he spilled back in the bin, with Vincent, another student helping. Brenda is ignoring everything but Martin and the homework paper in front of him. As in Florence Wang's room, she works to block out distractions for Martin.

Vincent has decided to stay on the floor under his desk after picking up the spilled pencils. He explains that he is annoyed because they were not supposed to read their journal entries aloud today, and his is not done. Now Gene joins Vincent in corroboration of the schedule and Brenda nods in agreement to confirm what the students are telling Regina. Regina seems flustered and announces that since they object to reading their journals aloud, there will now be a vocabulary quiz. Martin sees the quiz as punitive and bursts into song: "Whatcha gonna do? Bad boy, bad boy." Brenda cuts his song short very quietly and has him look her in the face as she talks to him. She switches from helping him with his homework to helping him write his name and the date on the top of the blank page for his vocabulary quiz. Regina asks Brenda if she is ready and she nods an affirmative.

The Paraeducator: The Other Grown-Up In The Classroom

Brenda scribes for Martin, who whispers his answers to her. Although he thinks he is whispering, I can hear him say: "period, adverb, comma, capital, paragraph, application", and I assume that the students in the class who are taking the same test can hear his answers as well. Martin gets louder but Brenda cautions him to talk more quietly and he does. He is done before the other four students and Brenda asks Regina if he can now read his book. Regina says "yes" and tells Martin "Good job." Brenda winks at me as Regina praises Martin, as if to say: "Who am I training?" The eye signal reminds me of the communication system I saw her use with Rachelle Delmont and Susan Compton. I am now an insider in her community of practice, but Regina is not.

Wednesday, April 30th and I am passing by the door to Shelley Plaistow's resource room. Brenda is sitting in the doorway, at a student's desk. She has sheets of paper on her desk and a black marker. She writes a message on one piece of paper and holds it up over her head, like an Olympics' judge. She is behind Martin, facing the teacher and he cannot see her signals. I found out later that she is letting the teacher know that Martin is out of bounds and what the teacher needs to do to correct his behavior. Brenda is trying to train the teacher to manage Martin's behavior so that he can be in her classroom without Brenda's support. Brenda is moving him towards independence in small group of five students. She initiated this process, showing agency at a level of independence far beyond that of the novice paraeducators.

With Ellen, I saw a paraeducator who was an outsider, but now I am observing a paraeducator who delineates her own community of practice with her student and herself in a central, included location. Her interpretation of the role is a different beast. The process is the same, however. Like her colleagues, Pat, Tiffany and

Ellen, Brenda observes, commits, communicates, adapts and partners.

Brenda's Process of Membership in the Classroom
Observe

Brenda asserts: "I pride myself that I am very good at observing people. And I was good at my job of nuclear medicine tech because I was good at observing people and knowing what was going to happen. I am good at watching facial expressions, knowing where they come from, what has happened, and if someone's in pain. Because of my experience, I know the signs that a lot of people may not be able to pick up: the signs from the eyes, the facial expression, maybe the body movement." Brenda looks at her work as requiring innate talent rather than credentials, marking the divide between schooling as a stratified, hierarchical process versus schooling as people performing social behaviors. The basis for her work, she believes, is her ability to observe.

"I know with Martin, all I have to do is look around our room and if I see that someone over there has dropped something, I know that within two seconds he'll pop out of his desk and try to pick that up for them. So I have to always know what's going on around me at all times: who is sneezing, who is talking, who is whispering, who is whistling, because he will pick up on all of that. Usually, if we are sitting there and someone is whistling across the room, I just go: (she demonstrates an enlargement of the eyes, and putting the mouth in a thin line.) I just give him that stare. Because I know within a few seconds, he just won't listen. I think it's being able to read the child psychologically, physically and to understand the classroom, to understand everything that's going on and being able to put it together in a split second and know what's going to happen."

She attests that observation is two way street. While she observes, she is being observed. She suspects that her reputation in the community of practice rests on observations teachers and administrators make about Martin's progress and behavior, not pleasing ancillary teachers. She said that she is pretty sure that her reputation rests on what the principal and administrators observe. "I think that when someone asks you: 'Who do you think would be good with this kid?' you can say: 'Brenda can deal with this kid. I know this is what she can handle. And this is the progress she will make for the child.' Because you've had discussions with the IAs, what they can handle, and what they have handled." She is certain that people observe and communicate.

Communicate

Observation is the start of her process, but observation serves communication. "And I talk a lot to the other kids in the classroom. They say, because I am the other adult in the classroom, the ones that are really comfortable with me will come and say things to me that they may not to the teacher. It's not that they wouldn't trust or go to Rachelle or to Susan Compton, but they see me all the time and they see how I work with Martin. If I were mean with Martin, they would back off. But if they see me as a comforting person, someone you can trust, they come to me a lot: 'Mrs. Carlsen, can I do this? Mrs. Carlsen, did you see this?'" Brenda talks about discourse with students, and how their observations of what she says and does creates their impression of her. The children and she build a history, interaction-by-interaction, conversation-by-conversation, that becomes their understanding of each other.

She illustrates that understanding by describing a social behavior, greeting. Communication starts at the beginning of the workday. "I go into Rachelle's classroom, and everyone says good morning to the kids. The kids say good morning to all of us. The whole room is a team. She tells the kids that these are your teachers just as I am. To show the same amount of respect and participate with them the way you would participate with me."

Brenda talks about negative experiences, with lack of communication. "We know that there are people here, that when the IA is in the room, they don't even want them to talk. You don't say anything, you are not to be heard, you just sit there until they need you." As a member of the larger school community of practice, I suspect that she is referencing the teacher Leslie Stands. But Brenda is discrete, and she never mentions her by name. "And I couldn't work with anybody like that, I couldn't do it. It wouldn't happen."

"I don't conduct myself in my job as if I'm just a caretaker. I probably take more responsibility, or I'm the type of person who is more assertive, than some I have seen in IA jobs. I had to tell Ms. Thompson 'You need to trust me enough to know that if I say he's not going to do something, he's not going to do it. I don't care how much you try to cajole him. I've been with him all day and he's finished, he's done, just done, that's it.' And that's one of the frustrations, too, probably is that when you go into the special areas people sometimes say: 'Well, if he would just' do this or that. He's not that kind of kid that 'if he would just'. When he's doing his own thing, he's off somewhere else and I perceive it to be my job to do what I can to pull him together so that he can listen to the teacher, so that he can interact appropriately in the classroom, and he can work with the other people." Throughout the story of her job, she communicates with students, teachers and administrators. She communicates in order to create a bond, or commitment between herself and others in the classroom and the school. Through communication, she is able to partner with teachers and students in order to adapt the school environment for her student so that he can learn.

Brenda states that sometimes, like Ellen, she is not kept informed. Like Ellen, Brenda fills the gap by seeking out people in the organization who have the information she needs. "Now, Paula [Martin's case manager on the Child Study Team] was very good. We had a meeting at the beginning of the year and she said: 'This is the child's problems' and 'This is our goal: make him more independent.' But no one says this is how you're going to do it. That's why I think you have to be very careful about which person you assign to the kid. As for you, you know each IA and as you get to know them, you know what they can handle what they can deal with, and the success that they've had with a variety of children. I was never really taught how to deal with Tami or Martin. It's just something I do."

Partnering is not possible, without communication sent and received. She and Regina may not agree, but at least Brenda is allowed to speak. She and Regina have a forced relationship for the school year. Brenda made a commitment to Regina, because she made a commitment to Martin.

Commit

"Martin knows what I am here for, because I tell him. 'I am here to make you successful, buddy. You're not cooperating with me. How can I make you successful if you don't want to try? I am here for you, so let's work together.'" Brenda continues: "You say: 'Okay I know how to deal with this kid. I know where they're coming from and I know what I need to do.' Basically, you come in and you're given an assignment. No one says what you do with that assignment."

"My main focus is my student. I don't always care if it bothers the teacher. That is my job, to take care of my student, not the teacher's ego. So, I do what I feel is best for my student. I never try to do anything to disrupt the class or to counter what the teacher has said or done unless they ask specifically for Martin to do something that I know at that particular point in time he is not capable of doing. It would be extremely stressful for him. So, I do what I feel is best for my student"

Brenda's commitment to her job parallels what she had learned in the health field. As a nuclear medicine technician, she was the expert in the hospital in her field for a patient. She is assigned to Martin because he has a problem, just as patients came to her at the hospital because they had a problem. She continues the theme of her superior understanding of the student as the source of her authority.

Based upon that authority, Brenda initiates several changes in classroom accommodations for Martin and actively arranges his relationship with one teacher to develop his independence. Although she is active and decisive, all the adaptations she creates are in reaction to the context the teachers create. Making a commitment to him leads her to attempt to adapt the learning environment and her own behavior, because Martin does not adapt easily.

Adapt

When Martin does not meet classroom demands, Brenda says that "I have to say, four and five times, 'Get your pencil out and put your name on the paper.' Or the teacher has given the instruction and he'll just sit there. 'Okay, Martin, Mrs. Delmonte says to put your name on the paper.' And of course, I have to be mindful of not talking too loud to interrupt her or to interrupt the kids who are around and doing things. We've gotten to the point that I let him know that if I say it three times you're really in trouble because that's inappropriate. Normally, what I do, I'll say it once—maybe he didn't hear me-I'll say it twice and then I'll go:

'Three, Two.' " She imitates Martin's voice. " 'Okay, okay, okay.' And that's what we do: count down. When our room is noisy, and our room is noisy when everybody is there and Rachelle and I both have a problem with noise ourselves. He definitely has a problem.

But that's what makes it difficult, when the room is sort of out of control. For example, in Mrs. Wang's class, when you do that hands-on thing, and the children can't help but talk and do things, Martin is just all over the place in his mind. You know he wants to go here and go there. And I'm just saying: 'No you have to stay here and complete this', 'you haven't completed that.' " She is the authority.

Adaptation comes at a cost to her: "There's a lot of stress that goes in to doing this job. There are times at the end of the day I can feel my eye twitching. You work so hard at keeping yourself together and working with that kid and there's a lot of stress that goes into working with these special kids one on one that no one ever understands. You can look at a kid from a distance, but until you have actually worked with them or know the person is working with them, you have no idea how stressful that can be." Often I have to use techniques to calm myself down and get myself centered and come across very calm and very straightforward. 'I am the boss, Martin and you need to listen to me.' Once he knows that I am that foundation for him, he can calm down. And when it doesn't work, we'll go out and take a walk, out in the hall or something." She outlines how she adapts herself to the stresses of working with Martin. She implicitly asserts the social self-control she needs to help Martin.

"If I say he's got to leave the classroom, he's got to leave. That's all there is to it. He's just not together and he's going to break down." Brenda feels stressed when a teacher makes expectations of her student that she perceives to be unrealistic.

Stress on Martin becomes pressure on her to coax, persuade and coach him to perform.

She coaches him to adapt his behavior. "I tell him: 'Just keep at it.' 'Pay attention.' 'Your teacher told you this.' 'Look at this.' 'Do that.'" And we get through things, until he has his little breakdowns. He doesn't get away with anything, I sit on him hard sometimes, and I don't let him backtalk me. I get right on him and say 'Totally inappropriate, do not talk to me that way again.' Everything I do is extremely consequential with a kid like this."

You want to feel like you're actually helping the child do something. For example, last year he did not have a successful year in gym. He had a very difficult time. And the gym teacher I think was a little reluctant to have Martin again. But, with Martin at the very beginning, I had to give him a lot of encouragement, saying: 'You can do it; I know you can do it.' I didn't really have to physically participate with him, but he would come to me and I would have to verbally encourage him, saying: 'thumbs up!' He developed self-confidence in gym in the beginning of the year and there has not been a problem with him in gym. He, as a matter of fact, looks forward to going to gym. And he will say: 'I'm doing great, aren't I?' And I will say 'You are doing wonderful in gym.'

"In science in the morning, when we go to Florence's class, that is really his first breakdown period. He has to really pay attention and he has to do teamwork. He cannot do teamwork. The classroom gets very noisy. Martin cannot handle noise. He'll look on the floor, and there's ants on the floor. He'll pick them up and he'll do all kinds of things. When we were just sitting and listening and taking notes, he was ok. I am having a difficult, difficult time with him in that class. He knows what the classroom is going to be like; he can't tolerate it. So, he doesn't do well. Last week, he didn't even make it to class. We sat in the library and we did our viruses and bacteria quietly." Brenda made the decision to have him learn the material out of the classroom, again evidencing her capacity to make decisions on her own on her student's behalf and adapting the learning environment, in this case a literal change in place, for her student.

Brenda works differently with each teacher but her role is the same. She secures resources and accommodations for Martin. She gauges when and where he is successful, using her understanding of what expectations he should meet in each community of practice. Brenda adapts.

Partner

"In the very beginning of the year, before the kids started, I didn't know who Rachelle was but I did know Susan (the other paraeducator assigned to the classroom). I had come in late the morning we were supposed to be here. I said: 'I'm supposed to be with Rachelle Delmonte, do you know who she is?' And Rachelle goes," Brenda uses a tone of great enthusiasm, " 'That's me!' And I said: 'Ok, well I'm with Martin.' And she said: 'O, thank heaven; I didn't know what I was going to do with all these kids.' Brenda laughed as she recalled their meeting for the first time. Brenda tells me this story, with evident pleasure, several times during the course of our discussions, both formally and informally. The story epitomizes several of her recurring themes: first, that she knows Rachelle needs her, and secondly, that Rachelle welcomes her as a partner.

"We bounce ideas off of each other, even sitting there in social studies. She's teaching the kids different things and she'll go: 'What about you, Mrs. Carlsen?' So, then I'll tell my experience and things I've done. She's not the individual who says: 'I'm the teacher and I'm the star.' She utilizes everyone in the classroom: 'What's your experience, what do you do?' She's even said it to the kids: 'my colleagues in this room and I'. Just a few minutes ago, when I needed to come here for this interview, I turned to Rachelle and said, 'I want to go talk to Mary. Is that OK?' She said: 'Yeah, he'll be OK, he'll sit and read.' Now, if it were me trying to walk out while she's trying to present social studies, she'd say, 'Can you wait?' So yeah, we would work that out." Through the story of this imagined discussion with Rachelle, Brenda depicts how they solve problems and make decisions as partners, but with the teacher the senior partner.[136]

She turns her thoughts to the resource room teacher who instructs Martin in math. "Shelley. We switched to her, so he was a little anxious about it. So I sat next to him and got his behavior under control. I said to her 'I'm going to start backing off. This is a class he could be very successful in.' And I'm just going to be putting a little strike for every time, a TRD.' I call it a Teacher Re-Direct anytime she has to tell him, very specifically, after she has given an instruction: 'Martin, pay attention' or 'Martin, do this.' And I write that down. And he's had very few redirects from the beginning from when I started backing off. I sat on the couch for about a week or two."

"Then I told her, 'I'm going to sit out at the desk, out in the doorway. I think he'll be just fine. There's no problem with him.' At the very beginning, he would look back to make sure I was there. Now, he knows I'm there and he's very successful in that class. And Shelley doesn't let him get away with anything. Every once in awhile, he'll do something. And I'll make a sign and hold it up. So she can see it over his head. 'This is what he needs to do; he needs to answer in a full sentence.' I told her, when he is capable of doing something, I let him do it." With this description,

---

[136] Geroux, 1997

Brenda demonstrates both her strong sense of agency and instances wherein she takes the lead as the expert on the child.

"I am on a colleague level, because I know my education level and I know my experience level. And I am right there with most of the teachers with college and experience, if not more advanced. I've never had anybody make me feel that I am less, although I know there is the potential for teachers to try to do that. I think they just don't know what the IA's [Instructional Assistant's] position is. I think some of them believe that the IA is a lesser person. They think they are their helper to do the grunt work, to do the photocopying, to do this and to do that, not as the colleague who is there to assist the kids.

Brenda, for all her frankness, is very careful not to give names of offending teachers, who by reputation from other paraeducators in the building, do not treat paraeducators with the respect that Brenda feels that deserve. She would, however, give the name of a teacher that I had seen her work with.

"I don't think classroom aides are responsible for making photocopies. They are responsible for helping the students, not doing the paperwork." Imitating Regina Thompson's voice, she says: " 'Well, last year the girl…' I said, 'I don't care what the aide did last year. I'm not the aide from last year.' And I said that I had spoken to Paula [Paula Thibeaux, the case manager on the child study team responsible for Martin] about this: 'I've spoken to Mrs. Thibeaux, and we both have the same understanding, is what I'm telling you. Martin is my job. I'm not here to hang your posters, to do your busy work, to do your photocopying.' I don't want to be mean about it, but that's not my job." She repeated herself for emphasis. "It's not my job." She addresses Regina and a host of imagined teachers: "I have probably as much education as any one of you do, and I'm not going to be treated like your maid." Brenda was clear on how the organization worked and felt that the school leaders could and should do more to define her job parameters: "And if it would come from the administration that these employees do not hang your artwork for you and they do not do your photocopying for you, that would improve things." Brenda did not use just her own beliefs to assert her position. She uses going up to the next level in the school hierarchy and speaking to the case manager to define her view of her role with Regina.

"And Regina is Regina. Then we get in her classroom and it's like 'ok, are we going to get anything done today?' We took- I keep saying we -Martin and I are symbiotic - the kids took their spelling test, once she found the sheet she needed to do the spelling from, which took a while. She didn't know where the vocabulary words were, so then they did something else while she found the vocabulary words and then they took the vocabulary test. When I get in there, I can't wait until two o'clock comes. Because I get anxious. 'Can we move this along? Can we move at a little faster pace? All the kids are starting to talk because you just need to move along." Brenda moves into another example of their difficulty partnering.

"I had a separate desk up through Christmas. Then, after Christmas, I go into the classroom and my desk is gone. Just the five students' have desks. I read that right off the bat, I knew what that meant." Brenda knows that having a desk displays membership in this community of practice. By taking away her desk, Regina was demoting her. As Wenger asserts, certain styles of behavior and certain artifacts convey membership.[137]

"So I just walked in, put my things down, I cleaned the crap off the chair that I could find, and sat back. And Regina goes 'Oh, I

---

[137] 1999

guess I don't have a desk for you here.' And I said, 'Oh, don't worry; I need to back off a little on him anyway. I think he'll be fine.' I think she was under the assumption that he could do a lot more than he was doing. That I was interfering with him being able to do the work. But she never discussed it with me. She never asked me or said: 'This is my feeling' or anything at all. " Lack of communication, again, prevents them from forming a partnership.

"So, after about four weeks or so, of just backing off on him, and he was getting up and down and being defiant with her and she wasn't getting anywhere and she goes [in high pitched drawl, imitating Regina]: " 'Well,' she says 'I understand that you want to back off on him a little bit, but I really need you to be more on top of it.' I said: 'Okay, whatever…whatever…I'll do it that way, that's fine.' Brenda is resigned but not passive. Brenda expresses her agency even in accepting Regina's unilateral decision, but it is the agency of reaction rather than initiation. She makes her observations of Martin, but again, communication fails with this teacher and they cannot partner effectively.

Her words are evidence of a community of practice because she believes that she and Regina have a sustained, if oftentimes negative, mutual relationship.[138] Brenda challenges Regina's notion of job hierarchy and power within the classroom. Brenda does not adapt her behavior to this classroom as much as she patrols the boundaries of her authority.

Brenda forms a partnership with her student Martin, which seems like its own community of practice that she attaches to each classroom. She is engaged in a community of practice as evidenced by her use and her creation of jargon, such as the "TRD's".[139] She is an insider by virtue of her track record: she worked well with a

---

[138] Ibid
[139] Wenger, 1999

student who is acknowledged by teachers and administrators to be extremely difficult.

Brenda let me know that many substitute teachers refuse to fill in for paraeducators. "I think the substitutes have finally figured out, 'those people have a tough job' because you know, you don't get a prep period. You are on your toes the whole time. The only thing you get, even if you don't get a full one, is your lunch. That is it. That's it.'"

Her reaction echoes Reich's suggestion that identity represents a resolution of the dialectic between the needs of self-identification and social identification.[140] Brenda regards herself as a worker doing a demanding job, not a person low on the school hierarchy. The substitutes' avoidance of her job validates her vision of her role as different from a teacher's but worthy of being a partner.

Summary

Brenda joins and sustains membership in communities of practice through a social process that is built upon social behaviors. She observes each classroom, communicates with teachers and students, makes a commitment to her role, and adapts the environment for her targeted student through partnering with the student and with teachers.

When I asserted that I saw a discrepancy between the published literature in this field and the observed characteristics of the participating paraeducators at Water Wheel School, Brenda was firmly in my mind's eye. Brenda's story about her relationship with teachers is confirming evidence that the nature of the occupation of paraeducator is dependent upon the relationship between the paraeducators and the teachers within that site. In her

---

[140] Reich, 2000

case however, she has created a community of practice that centers upon her relationship with her student and includes her relationship with the case manager. Both serve as a counterweight in her conflicted relationship with one teacher. Brenda envisions herself as a full partner with teachers. Her role with a student is different from a teacher's. "I think for what I do and the kids I work with I think it's something you have to have an instinct for. You can be trained to understand the difficulties each child has. You can be trained to know the definitions of what an ADD kid is or autism or anything of that nature but I think you have to have an intrinsic instinct of how to work with people like that. Not everyone can work with these kids. The classroom teachers can do classrooms, but I bet every one of them has said: 'I don't know how you do it with the kids that you work with because I couldn't do it.' It's sort of instinctual." With that statement, Brenda reveals that for her, teaching in a classroom is a different job than being a paraeducator.

She is not frustrated by the role, as are Pat and Ellen, who want to be teachers nor waiting patiently for a change, as is Tiffany. She relishes her role as she envisions that role. "I'm here for Martin. I'm here to make his year as successful as it can possibly be. That's my job." In order to help her student, she asserts the equality and sometimes superiority of her role in comparison to the classroom teacher's role. She is frustrated when some teachers, most notably Regina, do not recognize or agree with her definition of the role. She actively polices the boundaries of the role to make sure that she can fulfill her mission.

Daily, she maintains her place in the community of practice, as an expert who is the equal of teachers, through communication.[141]

---

[141] Sfard and Prusak, 2005

Her actions exemplify membership in a community of practice, but her focus is different from that of Pat, Tiffany and Ellen. She focuses upon her student more than the teachers and speaks with authority that emanates from her expertise with him.

She is self-motivated, but not by ambition to increase her status in the hierarchy by becoming a teacher. "You feel like you're really doing something for another person." She thought a bit and added: "I get to really know the kid and actually I get to know a lot of the other kids better, I think." She implies that "better" means better than the teachers. In her eyes, her status is comparable to but different from a teacher's, and she only needs people to acknowledge this fact.

Brenda finds that the job fulfills her need to do something beyond "staying at home", which was the need that prompted her return to work. Babs, too, returned to work after staying at home for years to raise a family.

Chapter Nine
Babs Bradford
A Job

Bab's Story of Self-identification

Babs is not the oldest paraeducator in the building. She informs me that one other is older at seventy, and last year, Opal Chevrolet was eighty-two and still working as a paraeducator fulltime. Babs sometimes needs things repeated, despite the help of her hearing aids. She is sixty-four.

Babs Bradford lives in a small town about a twenty-minute drive away from the school with her husband who has his own pest extermination business. They raised four children who are in their late thirties to early forties. She is a high school graduate with a few college credits. "I had to go to special classes to remain an instructional assistant," she reported. She was referring to the in-service training that the special services department offered four years ago to paraeducators who did not have two years of college credit.

Babs grew up in Baltimore. At the age of nineteen, she was working as a keypunch operator for a government agency when she met her husband, who was a Marine guard. "We got married and stayed in Maryland for a few years. And then he wanted to come back to beautiful New Jersey," she says with mild sarcasm. "When we came to New Jersey and we were in a second floor apartment. I said: 'I can look out and see a hundred miles.' Maryland is green and rolling and New Jersey is flat."

She returned to work when her children were young because: "You need two incomes to live in New Jersey. Our kids were getting older and college was looming." Babs has no desire to go to college herself, but wanted college for her children. A further impetus for employment was that her husband "was between jobs." For years prior to her reentry to the workforce, however, her husband had urged her to find work. She waited, she said: "I used to tell him that I do work, and told him once I started to work, it's going to be full time, too and for the rest of my life. That's what we did. He got a job, too. He was only between jobs. And I went into the secretarial field. I like to type."

She worked her way up from a typing pool to executive secretary for the director of commercial development in the local office of a national chemical company near her home. After twenty-four years of work as a secretary, her company was cutting back and she was asked to retire. "I was looking for jobs and they don't want older people and I was fifty-eight. People would call me in (for an interview) because they loved my resume. I can't say it was age discrimination, but I think that they hired people with less experience for less money."

Her friend, Anne DeSoto, encouraged her to apply for the position of paraeducator. Anne is a long time, well-respected social worker in one of the two middle schools. "She was talking to me about how the job hunt was going. She said: 'I think you'd be a good instructional assistant. 'Why don't you think about it?' I thought about it. I had another interview somewhere else and it went well, but no job offer. So, I said, well, I'll try being a paraeducator for a year. I said to her, 'I don't know how I'll be at this, but I'll try it out.' I went to the job interview and they hired me right away."

Babs, like Brenda, thinks that she came to the job with a good background and good natural talent. "Some of it is mother instinct or dealing with people, because I dealt with people as a secretary. And guided them and introduced them to Mr. Fax, when that came in." She laughed. "That's what I used to say cause the executives would say: 'Can you fax this?' And I would say, 'How about I introduce you to Mr. Fax?' So, I have been dealing with people. It's people skills, mostly."

She has been working as a paraeducator for five years. She is in the "senior" category with Brenda and Kelsey, but is the only paraeducator in the study who does not have an undergraduate degree. She received her training on the job and from her life and prior career experiences. She has a sponsor to help her into the district, with whom she maintains social ties. She sees herself as a worker who is something different than a teacher. She stays because she likes the job.

Babs in the Classroom

I try to schedule a day in January to see Babs in Cari Pearski's class, but Cari is reluctant to have me in her room this week. They are very busy she tells me.

February 21st at 11:05 and I am walking into Jena DeSale's class. Jena is scheduled to teach math to the students in Cari Pearski's class. I see Babs at the doorway, and she tells me that half of Cari's children attend Advanced and Enriched math class with Davis Brown. Despite that information, I am surprised to find so few students- seven - and so many adults - six. There is the teacher, three students from Walker College, a second paraeducator, Katherine and Babs. Jena is doing a lecture on geometry, so there is not much for any of the adults to do except to listen along with the students. The adults are sitting in a row of chairs behind the students, who are sitting on a rug on the classroom floor. Albert is reading a book, and Babs moves from her chair to sit beside him and quietly encourage him to close his book. She returns to her seat. The teacher continues to discuss transformations, reflections, rotations and translations.

Albert takes out a legal pad and pen and begins to write. Babs leaves her seat to rejoin him on the floor. Albert, I think, is writing the play he has been working on for months. He based the play upon a video game that he enjoys almost to the point of obsession. I was his case manager last year and know that his compulsions, like that of many children with on the autism spectrum, sometimes interfere with his attending to the teacher. Babs tries to get him to stop, but she deters him from his writing only momentarily. While Jena continues to discuss bases, faces and vertices, he writes. Babs tells him again to stop writing and to listen. Now the teacher is giving the children a follow-up written activity entitled "Where has Poly-gon?" Jena thinks that she is missing sheets. Babs takes the master and moves quickly towards the door to find a copier. Jena finds the papers after all and calls out: "Mrs. Bradford! I have the papers!" Babs returns to her seat.

As the children start to work independently, five adults: the two paraeducators, Babs and Katherine and the three Walker students, circulate through the room. The teacher, Jena, also starts to work with students one at a time. She tells me: "I like labs because they give me more one-on-one time with the kids. Babs and Katherine are good, too." Jena sees Babs as her helper so that she can teach, rather than a co-worker who also teaches. Babs performs supportive actions.

To complete the polygon activity the children need a wide range of crayon colors. Jena only has the basic eight colors in her crayon collection, but Babs remembers where there is a collection of pencils with the needed colors. She asks the teacher if she wants her to find those pencils and Jena says: "Sure." Babs exits the classroom. She returns quickly with several sets of colored pencils and distributes them to the students. She looks over the students' work, as do the other adults. Babs and Albert start talking about her help. Albert tells her that he wants her to "go away." She replies: "You need to have a good day if you want me to go away." After her discussion with him, she comes over to where I am sitting to tell me: "I usually don't sit so much."

It is the end of March, and I still want to see Babs in Cari Pearski's room, but I am having trouble doing that because whenever she is scheduled to be in Pearski's room, she is out on assignment somewhere in the building either walking the children to specials, taking the attendance to the main office or copying worksheets.

Thursday, April 24th, and it is Take Your Child to Work Day. Consequently, we have some extra children in the building who belong to the staff and we have some children absent who are presumably at work with their parents. In addition, we are in IEP (Individualized Educational Program) season. In this school, spring is the time for the annual meetings between the parents of children who are classified as eligible for special education and their teachers and case manager. During each meeting, the teachers and case manager review the child's progress and plan for the following year with the child's parents. While teachers are in the building during the meetings, they are not in the classrooms. So today there is a substitute teacher instructing the children in math in the resource room where Babs works for part of her day.

The resource room is half of one classroom, divided from the other half by a set of folding doors. There is one row of six desks, facing the green chalkboard on the folding wall. Babs sits between

151

two of the four children and they are all facing the instructor. A stranger to the school might be surprised at the diversity the scene presents: the substitute, Vyjaya Gupta is Indian, with a strong accent, one of the three girls, Shruti, is Indian, one girl, Sylvie, is Vietnamese, one girl, Cooper, is of European descent and the lone boy in the room, Raphael, is African American. One child, Brad, a boy of European descent, is absent. Babs seems to be in charge, because the substitute defers to her, and echoes what Babs says to the children. This echoing is something I have seen people new to the community of practice, like Pat, do. Babs in this case is the insider and Vyjaya, the outsider. Still, Babs manages to present herself as a support to Vyjaya.

Babs never corrects what the substitute says to the children, but tells the children several times what to do next. The substitute teacher reiterates Babs' directives. For example, when Cooper tries to answer "Nine times eight" and comes up with "Fifty-seven", Babs is the one who directs her to look up the answer in a multiplication table. The substitute echoes what Babs has said. Babs does all this while sitting with the children, in a child's seat. Babs models good behavior, and helps students sitting on either side of her. She also helps the substitute teacher who seems to be struggling with just how confused Cooper Bertolli is with the times table and how unwilling she is to give up her turn at the board writing problems. Babs tells Cooper to take turns, and Cooper relinquishes her spot.

Each child who subsequently gets a turn balks at giving it up. Babs talks in a quiet, calm voice to each child as they give up their turn at the board and take their seat. She checks on the whereabouts of one child who has been out at the bathroom for a very long time, and then traces a dollar sign in air to encourage Sylvie to put that in front of her answer on the board.

The Paraeducator: The Other Grown-Up In The Classroom

The resource room teacher, Betty Salvano, returns to her classroom to get something from her desk, and several children call out questions to her. Babs tells the children: "Mrs. Salvano is invisible, pretend she's not here", which they do. She does not give an introduction, a sign of a community of practice.[142] The period ends and the four children leave the classroom. Babs tells the substitute Vyjaya that the class went much easier "with that one out." She nods toward an empty desk, where Brad usually sits. She and Vyjaya discuss the child without referring to him by name, even though there are no children in the room who might overhear. Babs displays a verbal circumspection that is a hallmark of staff behavior in this school and thus a sign of membership in a community of practice.[143]

I think that the class ran smoothly because Babs is not out along with the teacher, although she would have a lot to contribute in the meetings with the parents. And of course, that is the perennial dilemma: who will supervise the children while the adults confer?

It is early May and Babs is out of Cari Pearski's classroom, looking for work to do because Cari says that she does not need her this period. She finds her colleague and fellow paraeducator Ellen, and they get a bulletin board to construct from Rick Johnson. She knows how to keep working and make her work socially pleasant.

It is June and there is field day. Cari gets sick and is out several days. I hear that Cari is getting married a week after school is out.. When she returns, she tells me that she only has a few days available. On several of those days, I have meetings with parents that I cannot postpone. We settle on one date, June 16th.

---

[142] Wenger, 1999
[143] Ibid

Unfortunately, she is out again on that day. As much as I would like to see Babs in that classroom, I need both Cari's permission and her presence. I never find a way into Cari's class to observe Babs there. I will have to rely on Babs' impression of the relationship, but I do regret not seeing them interact.

Babs was able to help the newcomer, the substitute teacher, function in the community of practice. She knows how to find appropriate tasks to keep herself useful. She displays the ability to assess the appropriateness of actions and products, which is characteristic of membership in a community of practice.[144] Her personal story and her experiences within the school give a context to her perceptions of her occupation.

Babs' Process of Membership in the Classroom
Observe

Babs reports that when she is in a classroom, she observes the teacher and the students for evidence that they need support. She says: "You have your antenna up, as you're sitting there, to see if anybody needs anything."

She recalls one time when helping many teachers was a problem. Babs is an experienced secretary, but when she used that skill, she got into a stressful situation two years ago. The key fact to understanding the problem is that secretaries are paid more than paraeducators. Babs was doing so much secretarial work for teachers and other staff members, that Belle Watson, the principal's secretary, noticed. Belle reported her observation to the principal with the understanding that if the principal could not redirect Babs, then Bell would go to the local union representative.

---

[144] Wenger, 1999

Babs discusses the incident: "I don't think it's a bad thing but I thought about that later. I was copying too much. And it didn't look good. I think they thought the teachers were putting too much on me. But it was when they were taking tests or when the students didn't need me. But we should be in the classroom with the students. I understand that. That was when the copiers were breaking down and I was coming up here and I thought that I was being watched." She reached a conclusion: "Just have to be more invisible."

Communicate

She considers her age both a hindrance and a blessing. She sometimes feels tired after a physical education class, but counters that lack of energy with the belief that her life experiences help her work with people. "Some of it you pick up along the way. Living with your husband day-to-day basis. That's a working relationship. I've been married forty-five years. We went to some marriage counseling. I had to learn to be more assertive. More defining of what I want. I don't mean in an awful way, in a stomp-your-foot way, this is what I want way. But more direct, I guess, is the word I'm looking for. And I worked on that. If you define and make a decision, it's easier with what you're doing. It makes you feel better about yourself. I feel good about myself most of the time." She prizes good communication skills and finds that she does better work because she has them.

Through communication with teachers, she learned her job. "Teachers are wonderful. I've been thinking about this since you were asking me to do this. And I was in with some teachers who were first year teachers, so we were working together. And I worked in the high school where they have a special ed group. I worked with these teachers in the classroom there."

She explains further: "Well some of the teachers would tell me afterwards, 'Mrs. Bradford,' Megan Rough, she's wonderful—she would say: 'Mrs. Bradford, I would like you to do this or not to do this'. It wasn't terrible things. I wasn't off the wall. She was guiding. I didn't quite know where I fit in, but they helped me to figure the job out and then, I could help them." Babs describes how she moved from outsider to insider, which mirrors Wenger's description of movement in a community of practice.[145]

She talks about emotional connections with the students as she had talked about emotional connections with the teachers. "Ok. Well, O'Malley's class loves me." Babs works in Maureen O'Malley's class one period each day as Pat's lunchtime relief. "They are so cute. I gave them Valentines this year. I made them like I did as a kid. You put a heart on top of a doily. And I just wrote 'Happy Valentine's Day'. They gave me hugs. And I wasn't even there that day because I think they were doing something. I just took the Valentine's down. And the next day when I saw them, they thought they were wonderful." She considers her other students. "And Albert and I seem to get along well. He's the one I work mostly with. He drew a picture the other day and gave it to me, because when he was drawing, I said: 'Is that a space ship? Is that a planet?' And I think he liked it because I recognized it. It was eighth period and they could do work or he could draw and he prefers to draw. He gave it to me and I took it home. I didn't put it on the fridge. I used to with my kids."

She continued to consider their relationship. "I mean there are times when I'm sure he hates me. There are times when I'm not sure I like him very much. But on the whole we seem to get along." Babs looks at her relationships through an emotional lens,

---

[145] Wenger, 1999

but while she is fond of certain students, she is clear that she does not have the same regard for them that she has for her own children and grandchildren.

"I try to use humor with the kids if it fits and other times just sit." Babs knows how to judge when an action on her part was appropriate within this community of practice.[146] "Different things work at different times. One good line is, 'if you don't get this done now, it's homework. And you don't want homework, do you?' I try to have lines, I guess. I did that with my kids too. If I had a good line, it seemed to work better. You could stick to it."

But for some children, her experience and her lines are not enough. "Brad is a whole other story. He and I seem to get along as well as anybody's going to get along with him. He does very well with Mrs. Salvano [a special education teacher], so I'll work with Raphael and Emily and whoever needs me. There are times when he allows me to help him. I don't think I've met a kid I really didn't like. I like kids. That's why we had four." Her schedule is fragmented like Ellen's and she has several classes in which she spends very little time. She concludes: "Because you're there just one period a week, you don't really see them much. But I'll go around and talk to kids, 'what are you doing?' They like telling me what they are doing. So, I try to be friendly and make a friend with them or you know at least appear to be a friend." She believes that she needed to connect socially with the students through discourse.

She sees herself as a support for the children's academic work. "They'll come to me if they want to go to the nurse, if the teacher is busy with somebody. I'll say: 'You have to ask.' Or, 'Oh, let's just wash that off and put a band-aid on that'. That's a kind of a

---

[146] Wenger,1999

trust thing. They trust me is what I'm saying. And that feels nice." Babs demonstrates a mutually defining identity with the students, that attests to her membership in a community of practice.[147]

Commit

I ask Babs if there was a student that she particularly likes working with and she has an immediate reply. "I worked with Sam," she says as if I should understand that he was a gem, and I do remember him. He was a bright, happy child with a mild case of cerebral palsy. She continues: "I was a one-on-one with him and it was like a second mother in a way. That's how I viewed it." Like Pat, Tiffany and Ellen, she felt that at times she has a close relationship with a child that is like a family member.

She acknowledges that she finds work with some other students to be difficult. Such as, "Sometimes getting them going if they don't want to. Kids can be stubborn and special ed kids can be really stubborn. They'll sharpen pencils and they'll move books around other than settle down and get started. I find that the most frustrating." She thinks for a while and says: "Sometimes a kid just looks at you and you know that the kid does not want to have anything to do with you because you are the authority or whatever. Sometimes, it's the anger, like Brad when I can't get into him. I think he is just mad at the world because he has trouble doing the schoolwork and he wants to be right all the time. Helping him is just hard. I don't know how to get to him. He's just an angry little boy and I feel sorry for him." Brad's anger prevents him from performing well in his role of student and prevents Babs from doing her role as his helper. As Wenger suggests, Babs and Brad have mutually defining, but not necessarily positive, identities.[148]

---

[147] Wenger, 1999
[148] 1999

Babs pauses for a minute and then remembers another child who is difficult to work with. "Albert has been better now, the past two weeks", she said with a smile. "He might be maturing. I don't mean he's perfect. But getting him focused is the main thing in class. Getting him started, once you get him started he seems to do all right. He has a hard time sitting and listening. The teacher in the class may ask, when she's giving a lesson: 'Albert, did you get that last part?' Or I sit by him, like that day you saw me. There's other kids in that class that seem to listen all right, but they seem to have problems once we get into the doing." Her understanding of him reveals inside information, characteristic of those who belong to a community of practice.[149]

Adapt

When I ask her what information she would give someone new to her job, she replies: "I'd tell them that the teachers are very organized. I'd tell them that their plans are together. And ask the teacher what they need, because what they need is different from period to period and from day to day. The students, too, are different from period to period and day to day at times." She sees her role in the community of practice as a fluid one that changes with the needs of the teachers and the students. I wonder if she sees herself as an emergency substitute teacher. She tells me: "No. Although at times, I do kind of teach a small group that's having problems." She reconsiders the use of the word "teach" and revises what she said. "Not really teach-teach. Maybe in math. Cause you can get down and really explain a problem again. I don't really feel like a substitute teacher. Sometimes I'll get a class started cause the teacher wants to run to the bathroom, because they're desperate. I'm there every day and when the subs are there, they

---

[149] Wenger, 1999

look towards me. I'm like the stable one. And I don't mean that in a bad way." Babs shapes part of her identity as the other adult via her constant presence in the classroom, ready to help when needed. It is a story she tells herself that shapes part of her identity.

She talks about the teachers with whom she works this year: "I worked with Mrs. Salvano last year and I love working with her again. Miss Pearski, I've been working with every year that I've been here. We are becoming friends now. There's an age difference. She'll tell me about things now, where before she didn't, quite. And I don't even know if she even thought that she wasn't, if that makes sense. But it seems as if she opened a door and let me come in. This is my third year with her." She believes that time had helped her build a relationship with this teacher.

"I like working with Mrs. DeSale. I just like the way she teaches math. But then I don't work with anything else with her other than that. I like working with Mrs. Teaberry, but it's different in social studies than it is in math. You sit and wait a lot. I like to be busy. With social studies, there is more sitting." Babs believes that her role changes with the subject being taught, the teaching style of each teacher and her relationship with each teacher. She is well aware of the variability of her job. "If you work with kids in anything you have to be adaptable, flexible, agile. All those words."

She gave the example of Albert. The teacher and the case manager came up with a plan to make Albert more independent because sixth grade is coming up. And I was involved in that after they discussed it. They told me what was expected. Because none of us can see him in sixth grade. I am sure it will be a disaster at first and then it will get better." Babs understands the appropriateness of behavior, another sign of membership in a community of practice.[150] Because she understands what is appropriate, she can help Albert adapt to expectations.

Partner

Babs says: "I've always felt part of the group. Here, the whole school feels that way. It takes a staff to do something to keep anything running smoothly." Babs entered the occupation believing that a paraeducator helps in the classroom. While she has increased her estimate of the level and value of that help, she has not changed her basic view of the occupation. Babs assesses her role with: "I think paraeducators are important in the classroom. Just as extra help with the students. More so than I thought when I became one."

Babs feels appreciated. "Well, the teachers are always thanking me, whether I do anything or not. 'Well, thank you Mrs. Bradford.' What's nice about the kids is that when we are walking in the hall from class to class, some of them will talk to me. I think that's nice. They will comment here or there: 'Mrs. Bradford, what do you think?' or whatever. It's people skills and connecting the adults. It's people wherever you turn."

She was the only participant to discuss her membership in a supportive group of fellow paraeducators. "Other instructional assistants, we're like a little family at times. And I don't know why that kind of happened but its seemed to have happened for me this year, my third year in this building. I felt comfortable last year but the first year I was a one-on-one and that keeps you a little more apart." Babs, unlike Ellen, sees her assignment to multiple communities of practice as a positive aspect of her job that integrates her more, rather than less, into the social network of the school. Perhaps her view is different from Ellen's because her

---

[150] Wenger, 1999.

level of work seems to be more akin to a support person than to an instructor.

Babs and the teachers have a mutual regard. "I grew up when you respected teachers and principals. My parents taught me that. They were the law. And I like what they do. I respect that. After having children of my own, I know how difficult it is to teach a child something sometimes when what you want to teach them is not just something they want to learn. And my children weren't bad, but they were normal kids."

Babs thinks that she gets along well with the teachers with whom she works. She says: "They all seem to like me. That's the way I feel about it. They all seem to like it when I come in and they will ask me to do things for them if they need it. That always feels good, when they rely upon me for something, like taking a kid out in the hall. I feel like I fit in. the teachers make me feel that I contribute to the workings of the classroom."

I ask her how many students she worked with in the course of a typical day. She answers: "There are four in Miss Pearski's room, and I'm with her mostly. There's one in Mrs. O'Malley's room. Mrs. Salvano's class there's six. That's the whole class. In Mrs. Savoy, there's just one, but he doesn't really need me." She is there as a medical precaution, in case the student has a seizure. "But I work with the whole class too, at times when they need help. If Jack's not having a problem in Mrs. O'Malley's, I go around to the other students if they raise their hands. I go around and help them if I can, if not they get in line for her." The children line up in a single file in front of Maureen O'Malley's desk so that they can speak to the teacher one at a time. "Cause sometimes they just need guidance. They just didn't quite get something." Babs defines her job in part as being there for backup, if the students do not understand the teacher's instruction.

The Paraeducator: The Other Grown-Up In The Classroom

Summary

Her way of helping the children do their academic work includes building a sustained mutual relationship, which is evidence of the existence of a community of practice.[151] "Getting along" and "liking" are words that Babs uses to describe her relationships with teachers and students. She acknowledges the children with Valentine's cards and they reciprocate with verbal thanks and physical hugs. As stated in the previous discussion of the underlying theoretical framework, Wenger suggests that there is a reciprocal process of ideas influencing actions and actions influencing identity. This process creates social space, role and identity.[152] In this case, Babs is the caregiver and the children are the recipients.

Babs envisions herself as a worker in the classroom who helps the teacher to teach the students to learn. She sees herself as an older worker with a wealth of useful life experiences as well as innate talent for the occupation. Babs says she learned how to be a paraeducator from teachers. She was hired when paraeducators only needed a high school diploma rather than the two years of college under current No Child Left Behind regulations. She fulfilled the education requirement through in-service classes offered by the East Brighton-Fieldtown school district.

Babs interprets her role in the community of practice through the lens of her past roles of secretary, wife and mother. She has a sense of where her practice fits into the larger scheme of school and the children's lives. She is able to assess the appropriateness of actions within the community of practice, which shows both that a

---

[151] Ibid
[152] Ibid, 1999.

community of practice exists and that she has membership in that practice.

She demonstrates how she interprets and resolves the ambiguity within the role through discourse of identity. She discusses how discourse with a sponsor eased her entrance into the occupation. She engages in discourse with teachers for role clarification and with teachers and students to bond with them.

She experienced tension and stress when she did "too much" photocopying, stretching too far into the role of secretary. The school secretaries felt she encroached on work they should be doing. She was very comfortable with this work, because she had been a secretary for many years before she became a paraeducator. Through discussion with the school principal, she changed her behavior.

She feels that the principal assigned her to her job based on her skills. "Well, you just choose people who you think are. Like anybody, some people fit better in a job than others." She, like Brenda, believes that she has innate talent for this occupation. She cites financial, social and emotional benefits to the job.

Although she is a senior member of this occupation in Water Wheel School, her work is more typical of a teacher's aide. She is sometimes superfluous if the teacher is in the classroom and can be spared to leave and search for needed materials. She does photocopy for the teachers, to excess according to the principal's secretary. Babs expects the teachers to let her know what they need, rather being a self-directed member of the classroom. She demonstrates the ambiguity within the role, which admits of a wide range of possible responses.[153]

Kelsey is the final participant in this study.

---

[153] Cornell, 2002

Chapter Ten
Kelsey Locke
Professional Para

Kelsey's Story of Self-identification

Kelsey has been working at Water Wheel for over four years, and in the district as a paraeducator for ten years. She is older than the three novices, but the youngest of the senior paraeducators. "My exact age as we speak is fifty-six. And I have my bachelor of arts in speech and language development and I do have my New Jersey teacher certificate in speech and language, kindergarten through grade twelve. Technically, I was trained to be a speech therapist. I went into college expecting to be a speech therapist and realized that I was more interested in the speech and language development from an educational point of view rather than sitting and helping children pronounce a proper 'p'. And so I got my certification, and then I taught for four years. I had fourth and fifth grade. Then I left. I was teaching in an inner city in East Orange, New Jersey."

Kelsey speaks slowly and with exactness, as if she has given some thought to the telling prior to the interview. Her hair is precisely cut into a chin length wedge, and she has her reading glasses on a beaded chain around her neck. She continues her story, giving context to her youthful career decisions.

"I was a classroom teacher. I actually did some teaching while I was in college. Now you have to go back to the seventies. It was a time when the campuses were always riled. I took advantage of the strike in seventy-one. When all of the campuses went on strike, my brothers and I traveled across country, to California. I got a summer job at a Montessori School. I didn't know anything about Montessori at all. I was basically there for their extended day. I saw all this interesting equipment and I was curious about what this was all about. When I came back, that was the summer of my freshman year in college, a person who was very involved in the American Montessori movement was offering a certification course at the Montclair adult school. A neighbor across the street said: 'Hey, you were working at that Montessori School, why don't we go and take this course and see what it is all about?' So we did, and at the end of the course, the instructor Nancy Brockman, offered us both a job at her nursery school. I started teaching the second half of my sophomore year in college. I was teaching a half-day in the preschool program.

That's really where I got started, you could say. I do come from a family of teachers. My father was professor of chemical engineering and my grandmother was a teacher. I guess you could say that I was exposed to it from the beginning. But I would say the Montessori School experience was the beginning. I have been teaching for all intents and purposes for a long time." Kelsey identifies herself as a teacher.

"I taught for four years and as I said it was an inner city school in East Orange. And just very physically, emotionally, mentally draining. Most of the time was spent basically just trying to keep peace ...so much time spent on discipline, just trying to get the kids to sit and listen. At the end of four years, I needed a break and I went into business to work for an insurance company. I was the liaison between businesses and the insurance company for employee benefits. After three years, I went to New York, working for a company that I had some contact with when I was working at the insurance company. Again became the liaison between the company and the insurance company. I got back into teaching in a way, because I had to do benefit seminars. I traveled around. Then, I had my children and realized that getting back into a school was the way to go so that I was on the same schedule as they were. And my personal circumstances were well suited to coming back as an assistant as opposed to a full time teacher." She notes that her husband's demanding (but she leaves unstated), well paying job in New York made it both desirable and possible for her to work part time. Kelsey sees herself as a teacher, albeit currently as a part-time, assistant teacher.

"When I got back into working as an assistant I started working at Hamlet— Hamlet school opened and I was helping out in the kindergarten and first grade. I guess I was there for about three years." Her work as a paraeducator was interrupted when her stepfather became gravely ill. "So I left for three years, and then I came back. Now I've been back for four and a half years. I came back to Gardiner Middle School mid-year as an instructional assistant assigned to the foreign language classes. I was replacing someone who had left and that's how I got back into it. At the end of that year, Martha Delacourt [who is currently a special education teacher at the Water Wheel School] was doing her student teaching and I was in one of the classes where she was. And we hit it off very well. When she was chosen to set up the autistic program here, she asked that I be an aide in her classroom. That's how I came to Water Wheel."

"I was just there, in Martha Delacourt's autistic class, for a year because I realized that that was not the best placement for me. I enjoy the interaction with the children and I just need feedback. And at the time the students that were in that class were pretty much non-communicative and I basically said to her: 'I'm here, I'll help you with your first year, but this is not really where I want to stay.' Then, I was with Leslie Stands. I did a year there."

Without having to say much and only giving a look, she conveys how difficult a year with Leslie Stands was. Leslie is a special education teacher who some school personal, including myself, find rigid and socially awkward. Leslie often complains that no paraeducator stays with her for more than a school year. In fact, many only stay for a few months. Leslie attributes this loss to the administration that unaccountably lets other paraeducators remain with the same teacher year after year. What Leslie does not seem to understand is that each paraeducator who works with her requests an assignment change. Staying a full year in Leslie's class is an accomplishment.

Kelsey went on to say: "Then, there was an opening in Sharon Killigan's class as a one-on-one for Aaron." Sharon Killigan, who sponsored Brenda, teaches children who are cognitively impaired who often require one-to-one aides. Aaron is a young boy with Down syndrome who needed close supervision throughout the day. "I shifted then from being a classroom aide to then doing a one-on-one which I did for two years with Aaron and now I'm doing with Hamish." Hamish is in a general education class all day while Aaron was in a special education class all day. From her point of view there is not a distinction between the two assignments.

Kelsey has some views and values in common with other paraeducators. She, like Pat, Babs, Brenda and Tiffany, feels that she entered the job with ease. Her sponsor is in her school. The interview questions led her to discuss her credentials: a college degree and a teaching certificate. She notes her years of experience as a paraeducator in this school building. Like Ellen and Tiffany, having a husband and children was an important part of how she sees herself and a source of pride. She considers herself a teacher, albeit assisting and part-time. She also has done other types of work and is satisfied to have made this occupation her choice. Her current position of paraeducator is her career destination.

Kelsey in the Classroom

February 28th, at 8:15 a.m. and I am in Gretchen's classroom. I am talking to both Gretchen and Kelsey about the upcoming state test administration for Hamish, who has autism. Kelsey is his one-to-one assistant. His last year's teacher, who is also Kelsey's sponsor, Margaret Delacourt, is concerned that he would not be able to fill in the information sheet. We start talking about his perfectionism. Kelsey tells us that Hamish has a hard time with the "mad minute" every Wednesday. The "mad minute" is a sheet of math computations which students typically do one time per week for two minutes, week after week, to so improve their speed of recalling math facts. Hamish, according to Kelsey, gets furious when he can't complete the sheet. He thinks that he is supposed to do it all. Gretchen says that no one in the class can complete the sheet in two minutes. Gretchen comments: "Wednesdays must suck for Hamish, then." Gretchen decides that she can put a mark where he completed the computations the week prior and say this is where he should get to on his next attempt.

Kelsey and Gretchen seem to have a nice rapport. I think that an outsider would find it hard to distinguish who is the teacher and who is the assistant. Kelsey is Gretchen's senior by about twenty years and dresses neatly in a green matching sweater and slacks set, with a tidy scarf. Gretchen, like some of the other teachers, is dressed in a peasant skirt and Birkenstocks. Dress is not a marker to distinguish roles. Gretchen and Kelsey speak as equals and are equally deferential to each other.

Kelsey leaves the room with me, because she wants to see how Hamish has arrived. By "how he has arrived", Kelsey means his emotional state rather than his mode of transportation. His grandfather had bypass surgery yesterday and the family has been spending part of every day over the past few days at the hospital. He has the added stress of a part in an upcoming class play, which is part improvisation. Children with autism are known for needing sameness and routine. Both events have changed his schedule. "Although he is doing very well," she adds. She just doesn't want him to come into the classroom in tears if he has had a substitute bus driver, which is his usual response if there is that change to his routine. Kelsey would rather greet him in the hall and calm him down if need be before he arrives in the classroom. After all, she tells me, "He is only nine." Kelsey displays her knowledge of the expectations of this community of practice that Hamish should avoid breaking.[154]

She passes Brenda, another paraeducator, and jokes: "A better hair day!" Brenda responds with: "I actually did something with it today." They both laugh, although I am not sure why. Kelsey and Brenda demonstrate another hallmark of mutual membership in a community of practice: inside jokes.[155]

Hamish sails by looking calm. Kelsey yells "Hello" to Hamish as a classmate is calling: "Hamish, Hamish." Hamish goes to class with his friend, and Kelsey trails behind him at a discrete distance.

February 29th, at 10:25 in the morning and Ms. Gretchen Sontag's class is about to present a play in the multipurpose room for Black History Month. They have been rehearsing since they returned from the holiday break in early January. The title of the play is emblazoned on a banner across the bottom of the stage, "The Courage of Frederick Douglass." There are about two hundred children and adults in the audience, to whom Gretchen explains the reason for the play and makes introductions. The

---

[154] Wenger, 1999
[155] Ibid

twenty-four children waiting on stage are dressed in black and barefoot. The play begins. The children drum, dance, and do choral reading as well as speak individual lines. The children say their lines in a variety of accents, including French, Korean, Spanish and Chinese. Gretchen has the ESL (English as a Second Language) class students who leave her classroom for part of the day to receive instruction from the ESL teacher. These same children entered her class in September not speaking any English and she concentrates on choral reading and plays to help them acquire the language. But I am not here to see the play, although my eyes often shift back to the compelling performance on stage. I am here to observe Kelsey.

Kelsey is in the back of the cafeteria/auditorium, behind the rows of chairs, with a camera on a tripod, videotaping the show. She watches the production through the lens of her camera, standing throughout and focused on her task for the twenty minutes it lasts. She is the first to start clapping, to signal the end of the production. The crowd of family and students join her and clap enthusiastically, too.

After the children and the teacher take their bows, a reporter from the local paper interviews Gretchen, while Kelsey starts to pick up the props. The children are all in the audience now, talking to their parents, grandparents, and assorted other relatives. Gretchen mouths "Thank you" silently to Kelsey, which Kelsey acknowledges with a smile and a nod. This short cut to communication is typical of behavior in a community of practice.[156]

The two custodians are rearranging the chairs and pulling out tables from the sides of the room, to change the room from a

---

[156] Wenger, 1999.

theater to a cafeteria. First lunch starts in fifteen minutes. Sally Gold, a paraeducator who has been watching the production with some students from another class, congratulates Kelsey. Kelsey tells her: "They did very well." The good performance is understood by her fellow paraeducator as an achievement and a source of justifiable pride. Shared understanding is also evidence of a community of practice.[157]

The custodians rush around with chairs, the parents chat, teachers lead their students back to class, and Gretchen poses for the photographer who accompanies the reporter while Kelsey takes the speakers off the stage, and winds up the cords from the microphones. Both she and Gretchen demonstrate the difference between their roles and their mutual understanding of those differences. They each have their negotiated place in the community of practice.[158]

April 22nd, at about 9:35, when I enter Gretchen and Kelsey's classroom. Kelsey is talking to the teacher of Chinese about Hamish's difficulty learning Chinese. As soon as I slip in the door, Cynthia Hunter is right behind me. Cynthia was a principal in the district seven years ago and now supervises the very small student teaching program at nearby exclusive Ivytown University. Gretchen is hosting a potential student teacher in the program. Usually, when a teacher is pulled from attending to a class by a visiting adult, the children get restless, but that does not happen with Kelsey in Ms. Sontag's room. As soon as Kelsey sees that Cynthia has pulled Gretchen's attention from the class, she completes her discussion with the teacher of Chinese and picks up the discussion Gretchen was having with the children. Some children ignore her. She pulls out a whistle and blows a shrill

---

[157] Wenger, 1999
[158] Ibid

"toot!" She says in a loud voice: "What should you do when the whistle blows?" The children become silent and a few lift their hands to volunteer an answer. Kelsey starts a discussion with: "How do you handle rumors?" I hear Cynthia murmur to Gretchen that she is "so lucky to have Kelsey." Kelsey tells the children: "You don't pass it on, or even listen to it. We will talk about it more, because you are confronted with it every day." Kelsey's discourse with the entire class is directive. Kelsey is the disciplinarian in the classroom, unlike the other five observed paraeducators.

Gretchen leans over to me to whisper: "Every IA (instructional assistant) should be a teacher." Meanwhile, Kelsey continues her discussion with the class. Vincent laughs out of turn and she gives him a severe look, but passes on to Arvin and calls his name. "Arvin, what are you doing?" Arvin is evidently throwing his study guides into the trashcan. Kelsey handles that problem as well by having him pull them out. This behavior is teacher behavior and I conclude that she and Gretchen are co-teaching.

Later that same day, during activity period, I look for Kelsey in order to arrange a time for an interview. It is the end of the day and Gretchen tells me that Kelsey is with Hamish in orchestra. The orchestra is rehearsing for their upcoming concert on the stage in the multi-purpose room that doubles as cafeteria and theater. I stand in the cafeteria area, scanning the stage for Kelsey, but do not see her. I spy Hamish, who is sitting with his cello propped between his legs at the far lower right of the stage. He seems to be staring straight at me while he is bowing his instrument, but I follow his gaze and realize he is looking above me at the clock over my head. He averts his head away from the music and the conductor, but he saws the bow back and forth. I see a movement of the curtains behind him. Kelsey is hiding behind the curtain and holding his elbow to prompt him to bow the cello. I think that the moment is a good metaphor for her role. She is privately and unobtrusively behind the scenes enhancing what others do publicly.

Her interactions with Gretchen are hard to catch, because they are so subtle and so quick. She seems to know what Gretchen and the children need almost before they need it. She anticipates events and smoothes the way. Her skill supporting a teacher or a student is so facile that it is hard to catch without focusing carefully on her and her alone. Much is done without words. She understands implicitly what was to be done in the setting. Both the lack of words and the sense of what is acceptable are signs of membership in a community of practice.[159] Her teacher considers her to be a colleague and thinks that all paraeducators should have Kelsey's level of training and expertise. Her story illustrates one way an experienced paraeducator works in an elementary classroom. The observations give a context to her views of her role.

Kelsey's Process of Membership in the Classroom
Observe

Kelsey discusses her deliberate approach to each new assignment. "If this is the very first time I am coming into a class, I spend the first couple of minutes just trying to observe and listen. What are you hearing the kids saying? What do you see going on? To watch. I don't just come in and focus on, 'here is the schedule, here is the lesson'. I look at them as individuals, look at them as people. Observe them. And that will help me to get through the day. They may say something that I can connect with. And I say, 'Hi, I am so and so, that reminds me, I have a dog, too, yadda,

---

[159] Wenger 1999

yadda' so I become more personable to them that I'm not just this thing standing on the side of the room, sort of cold and unapproachable. I think the first thing, coming in cold, is just to step back and observe." Kelsey plans her actions as reactions to the members of the classroom.

She also talks about the targeted children that she has worked with as a one-to-one over the years. "When you are doing a one-on-one, you really have to key in on that one child. Understanding the nature of the problem and then how do you help that child fit into the situation. Your focus then is really on the one child not the twenty-five others in the class. And you really need to watch them. Pay attention to what is going on, how the other children are relating to him and how they are relating to the other children. You really need to focus on them and watch everything that's going on because you are trying to perceive it the way they are and how to help them deal with their situation-so you almost have to [say]: 'so if I was ten and somebody said that to me, or I had to do this when I was ten, how would I approach it?' Particularly if you have to adapt some of the subject matter in the academic side of things but even socially, how they interact socially."

Communicate

"I love having conversations with the students. I'll hear something and then I just turn around and jump into a conversation." She recalls her recent experience with the children performing in the play: "It was great, it was great. It was a wonderful experience, watching the students, since half of those children did not speak English when they started school in September. To see the look on their faces. I was getting emotional as each one came up to the microphone. You could see the growth."

175

"I love the job, I love the kids. The kids come to me from time to time and we will have private conversations. If I have a conversation with a child, I make sure that I tell the teacher about it." She links the children and the teacher.

She worked with students all the time, anywhere in the school. "In the cafeteria. Pretty much wherever I am. If you see things, or kids will come up to you if they need mediation. I am sure the other kids in there think I am one of the lunch aides, so they tend to come up, I tend to get involved. If I see somebody doing something where somebody might be getting hurt, I will intervene. I don't just focus on the one child. I don't know technically if that's ok. We're here basically to bring children along. And you would never know if you looked in the window that he is different from the other children."

I query her on what helps her build relationships with the students and she says: "You know, I love to talk with the kids, just to have a quick: 'How was your weekend? How was your evening?' I'll share things with them about my family: 'Oh, you won't believe what happened to me over the weekend.' And that generates a conversation. It's those moments where you can talk to them one-on-one just about them and what's going on in their life that makes connections. I think it's helpful to them when you do have to make, maybe reprimand them, they are comfortable with you, they accept you, they know they can trust you. They'll tell you things and ask you not to say anything, so you try to, you know." Discourse was important in creating her bond with the children.

For the past few years, Kelsey has worked with students who spend their days with one academic teacher, with only one period away from that teacher daily for an elective such as music or computer class. She does not do lunch and recess duty. As a result, she spends more time with one teacher than any other participant in the study.

Kelsey reports that she enjoys working with the teachers as colleagues and enjoys the experiences and the friendships that developed from that work. She connects with people at work through talking about outside interests. She also signs up for conferences with the teachers. In addition, she joined a book club for teachers in the school. She likes and admires teachers as people and enjoys having them as friends. Many of these activities are outside the normal bounds of her job description and working hours. These activities give her additional time to bond with the teachers.

She also creates bonds with the students. "Certain students have problems with focusing and attention, so trying quietly to be near them, remind them what they are supposed to be doing, maybe taking notes: 'What do you need? And where would you find it? If you need a pencil, where could you find a pencil?' Just sort of helping them along to working them through the steps to get them through a particular lesson. It's rare that I find a student that I can't find something good or enjoyable about them. It's rare. I think if you look deep enough you can find something you like about that child. And that comes from having conversations with them and I think sort of dealing with them as people. Not just in that traditional, I'm the teacher, you're the student. It's that they hear that you have a life outside of school, that things are going on and you share those. Once those connections are made, you can help them. It's about getting their trust. They know that they can talk to you, that they can come to you, that they can seek you out."

Commit

Kelsey sees herself as on assignment with particular people: "I look at the classroom more as the classroom teacher's. That's their domain. I am in there to help. I'm coming in here every day for 180 days, so I want to be friends and if I can't be that, then at least friendly. I approach it each year: this is my assignment for the year. How can I make it work? I have never asked mid-year to be changed. I have not asked to be reassigned. Whatever I am assigned, that's my job for the year."

Kelsey says that she had a year where she was tempted to ask for a reassignment, but did not do so. And she is proud of her ability to stay with a student or a teacher for the ten months of the school year. Kelsey talks about her toughest year as a paraeducator, which was the year that she worked with Leslie Stands. "There were about six (students) that year. Two of them that year went out for science. You know, sometimes you can see the kids need to rest. I'm the kind of person who will share information, if I have a conversation with a child. But I wasn't really allowed to do anything. I was not allowed to do any monitoring, other than something like: 'Can you make sure he closes his book before we do the test?' Because of control. That particular individual cannot give up any control. I lasted the full year. I wonder what people were thinking of me when I asked to be reassigned."

I tell her: "Oh, I don't think people were thinking anything about *you*." I remembered people wondering how long she would last in that room. The teacher had a lengthy history of difficulty working with other staff members as well as paraeducators. Kelsey laughs: "Well they did try more people. I think they wanted to see if a person with a different personality would be able to work with her. But you could put anyone in there…" her voice trailed off, and we both mentally completed the unspoken end of the sentence: "and they would have a hard time.'"

I ask her if she and Gretchen had a conversation in the beginning of the year to decide how they were going to divide their duties. She thinks for a moment and says: "No. Although I tried that in the other situation. And I thought that after having a conversation, something would change. But it didn't. She has her routines."

"I do feel that the experience with that teacher was odd. It was interesting. By and large people get along and I think that's the way it is in any organization. In business, they'd just get rid of them, but here tenure keeps them on board. It's not the type of job a person can do who is not social. I never had anything like that before and probably will never again. You know there are definitely other people out there who are controlling, but not like that." The school year she worked with Leslie Stands she regarded as an anomaly. She has given this difficult relationship with a teacher thought, even though it is two years in the past. She integrates that experience into her identity.[160]

"I would probably say that Gretchen is a direct opposite. It's a little bit different because technically I'm a one to one this year; I'm not the general classroom aide but for all intents and purposes that's how I function. I think that once the teachers see that you're there to help them, you're not there competing with them, once you work together for a while, you build something." That something would be membership in a mutual community of practice according to Wenger's definition.[161]

Adapt

Kelsey talks about the students she currently works with in Gretchen's room: "There are an eclectic mix, all different learning styles, in that particular class, you have other languages. There's

---

[160] Fitch, 2003
[161] 1999

ten ESL students in there and each one of them has their own background and their own baggage that they bring into school every day. How do you connect with them on a day-to-day basis and get across the curriculum that you are supposed to get across? At any given moment, you only have maybe about ten of them paying attention" she laughs. "No matter how great the lesson is. So, just trying to keep them on focus and paying attention and hopefully learning something each day."

Kelsey looks at her work with students as supportive and in reaction to their needs. "If I'm sort of circling around, I see what needs to be done. It's like having another kid in the class, if you always have to be told what to do. Sometimes, you have kids where they will ask for something. One of the kids will ask to go to the bathroom and I'll say 'yes', without realizing that the teacher was about to start something. I don't have a problem saying: 'You know what, the teacher wants you to stay in the class, I didn't realize that.' I want to melt into the classroom, not stand out." Kelsey presumes that she knows what needs to be done and how to do it, so she does it with little direction and in the background. She knows that she has changed in the role over time: "I used to be asked to do a lot of clerical work, like photocopying. You know, I just see what needs to be done. I'm pretty secure with myself. I don't need to go into these classrooms, looking for something." Kelsey adapts to her background.

Partner

Kelsey defines herself as a kind of teacher, which influences how she perceives the teachers with whom she works. "I see it [the occupation] as an assistant teacher. The classroom teacher sets about presenting information and I look at it, as how can I support that teacher? How can I help that teacher get across what she, he or she is trying to accomplish? So while the lesson is going on, I'm thinking, is there something that I can help her with? Is she talking about something where maybe there is a piece of equipment in the room that maybe I can just quickly get and hand to her so that she doesn't have to stop? For instance, if you were talking about geographical terms or whatever, and children started to ask various questions, I could go and just grab the globe and bring it over. To help support her, so that they'd have a visual. I'm always trying to anticipate what's coming next; how I can add to what she is doing, help her? So I look at it as what can I be doing so that I can support what is being presented, so that she doesn't have to stop and interrupt the flow of the lesson. The other side of it is, somebody gets a bloody nose, somebody can't find their paper, that kind of thing, and I can deal with those issues so that she can keep going with the lesson."

"My teaching experience made it easy to anticipate what's coming. You have been through presenting information to children, you've done lesson plans so you know the kinds of things that you need. It does make it easier." Kelsey tells a story of how she came to her current job by explaining how she became interested in teaching. She again reveals that she considers herself to be a teacher. Ideas influence practice and the proactive influences ideas.[162]

She likes working with Gretchen. I comment that I saw Gretchen trading looks with her and it was a very quick communication that an outsider would find hard to catch. "Because I knew what she wanted. That's the beauty of being with someone all day and all year." They have established roles that seemed clear to me and certainly clear to them. Kelsey is the disciplinarian the majority of the time, and Gretchen is the creative force, which was

---

[162] Wenger, 1999

evident when they were rehearsing the play. I ventured my view of the division of labor with Kelsey, and she rejoined: "Right. Exactly. Gretchen would say to me: 'This is great. You're able to focus on that type of stuff, and I'm able to focus on the creative things.' And she does, she can look at the whole thing and focus on the music, and the movement." Kelsey admires Gretchen's work, giving her a high accolade: "This teacher is very professional. She is so in tune with those children and she knows what they need. There are some teachers who teach by the book and that is not necessarily bad. They just don't go beyond what is in the book or adapt it for the children in their classroom. But Gretchen does."

Kelsey considers the children's lives outside of school when she works with them in class: "They have their life here at school, they have their life at home. There are a lot of things going on in their homes that we can't control and you can see sometimes the impact in the classrooms. You are really not at liberty to get into a discussion about it, only if they have shared some things with you. That can be difficult. To know that they are bringing their anger, their frustration from home and there is only so much that you can say to them about it." Kelsey regards boundaries to the support she can give children as a reality of her community of practice. She resolves the pull between her personal and social self by acknowledging those limits, and having discourse with the students to make social bonds appropriate to the community of practice.

Summary

Kelsey is a paraeducator who works as an assisting teacher in the general education classroom. She is aware that her level of training is beyond the expected. "This district is lucky because many of the aides have a teaching degree or they have had experience with teaching, which I think is unusual. I think in most school districts, it's whoever they can get in to do the job. A lot of the instructional assistants live in the town. Their children are going through the school system so you have people who are interested. This is our school district. So you have a vested interest in making sure that things are working well and the kids are getting the attention that they need. I think that is a big plus. I don't think that that necessarily happens in a lot of other places. I think it works well."

Kelsey learned how to be a paraeducator, she believes, through formal teacher training in both Montessori methods and speech and language therapy methods. She also attributes her learning the job to self-reflective and collaborative experiences in the classroom. She believes that she has innate talents and interests, such as her social ability, that helped her learn how to perform the job.

She approaches the job from a stance of whole-hearted involvement. "I think, as with any job, you can come in and just literally do what's written on the job description. I have never approached jobs that way. It's always, yes, here is the basic description of what I do, but are there other things I can do, other things I can read, other things I can go and experience that will enrich the whole package. I am always trying to learn new things. Even when I wasn't here and I was with my ill parent, I was still asking the teachers: 'What are the current topics? What are the books you are being asked to read?' I would borrow them and read them. I am always trying to stay current. That's what I do. I assume that that helps. If the students are in a concert, I will make an effort to come and see them. Little things like that. Those are extra and above and beyond and I am able to do that, I am in a position where I can come back and do those extra things or take a course somewhere. Not everybody can do that. I am pretty fortunate that I've been able to do that."

Chapter 10:   Kelsey Locke Professional Para

Kelsey values the work hours that are shorter than a teacher's and school vacations that parallel her children's schedules as rewards of the occupation: "My personal circumstances were well suited to coming back as an assistant as opposed to a full time teacher. You come, you're here. You do your job while you're here. At the end of the day, you don't have to do a lot of the paperwork, a lot of contact with the parents. That mainly was the biggest difference and that was just the area that allowed me to do what I need to do for my family. As a teacher, the day doesn't end at three o'clock. That was the difference for me."

Rather than being less financially secure than the teachers, Kelsey, like Ellen and Brenda may be more financially secure than many teachers. They could afford to work fewer hours for less money. She explains: "My husband was working in the city and very long hours. Left very early in the morning and came home very late. I needed to be around for the children. It was great to be on the same schedule, to have the same snow days, the same vacation days. It just worked perfectly. Then when I left school at three, I was just able to concentrate on them when I got home. I didn't have all the extra lesson plans, the paperwork, the parent contact, and so forth. I was fortunate enough that this was not going to be a main source of income for us. I just love interacting with the children. I love watching the way kids learn and I love to see their growth, their personalities."

Kelsey's approach to the job is at first glance a paradox: she will do above and beyond what is expected of a paraeducator. She does the "above and beyond", however, within her schedule that allows her to put the care of her own children as a priority. When asked what she considers to be the pluses of the occupation, she reiterates that she enjoys the time she spends with children and teachers.

The Paraeducator: The Other Grown-Up In The Classroom

The evidence supports that conclusion. She is working within a community of practice and is an integral member of that community. Kelsey uses discourse to clarify her role and create social bonds. She feels strongly about the social value of her chosen occupation. "I think it always comes back to, is it a job or is it something you really like to do? I just love it. I wake up everyday and I'm excited about coming in. Something new is going to happen every day. You know, this isn't just as an aide, it goes across the board: you need to love what you're doing. You might be able to say 'I can get a job at McDonald's' and work so many hours and get paid. You can work by yourself and just deal with the person across the counter. Working with kids in school, you can't just take it as a job. You have such an impact on them while you have them that you really shouldn't be getting into it unless you really enjoy working with kids. I think you can see sometimes when people come in and it's just a job. I think you can tell right away. The kids don't relate to them. That's all. It either works or it doesn't work. The nature of the job is to be social.

Chapter Eleven
Measuring and Meaning

Outside Confirming Evidence

In any small study such as this one, the chance selection of participants could lead to a skewed perspective. Perhaps the paraeducators engaged as participants have an unrealistic view of their responsibilities. Outside confirming evidence is supportive.

Seven years ago, when the presence of paraeducators started to look like a permanent part of programming for special education students, one of the members of an elementary school child study team created a list of all the duties a paraeducator could perform. The social worker took these duties from lists, books and IEP documents she and others had developed. Kate Spinnings, the special education supervisor, read this document and distributed an electronic copy to each social worker, psychologist and learning disabilities consultant in the district. Each child study team member now highlights a handful of major tasks that the paraeducator will do for a student.

The headings are encompassing: modifications in the mainstream classroom, reading, writing, math, science/social studies, organization, attention, and behavior. When I analyze the language employed in the text, especially the verbs, I construe a sense of a subordinate position with little agency. For example, "encourage student to" appears twenty-two times within the list. "Help student" appears sixteen times. The words "allow", "prepare student", "monitor", "support", "assist" and "provide" are peppered throughout the document. Direct action is, as expected, based upon student behavior. For example, "gradually lengthen written output expectations as student is able to produce more written work", "take up student's work as soon as it is completed," and "give a 'five minute warning' etc. to help student manage time effectively." The language that a child study team member uses in this document confirms the outside locus of control that the participants report. The length and breadth of the document also supports the wide range of possible needs the paraeducator may be asked to undertake, depending upon the needs of the student.

Synopsis and Review of Identities

When I reviewed the literature in this field, I noted that many researchers found that role confusion and lack of training are endemic problems for paraeducators. The purpose of this study is to look at how a group of paraeducators in a well-resourced school district define their occupation and to see if they, too, find themselves confused in their role and in need of more training. The selected group has a range of training and all six have experience in schools as either teachers or paraeducators. If these privileged members of this occupation in this well-resourced place have difficulties, I could reasonably deduce that the problems may lie elsewhere than in themselves.

The six paraeducator participants answered the research questions by talking about their identity through their personal history and their self-defined relationships with teachers and students. From a review of relevant literature, I hypothesized that the paraeducators entered and sustained their membership into classrooms through a community of practice. I observed the participants at work and interviewed them for evidence to support my supposition. Through their words and actions, they answered the research questions. Review of these answers revealed a cohesive understanding of their occupation.

Chapter 11: Measuring and Meaning

Who are the paraeducators at Water Wheel School? The broad answer to the first research question is: they are collections of individuals, all female, who work with children in classrooms. I review each paraeducator's self-discourse outlining her current view of herself and her occupation for purposes of this discussion.

Pat identifies herself as hardworking and ambitious in her discourse. She has an undergraduate degree in communication and courses towards her masters in sports administration. She had taught in private school so had previous experience in a classroom. She plans to attain a higher status within the school hierarchy by getting a teaching certificate in order to meet her ultimate career goal to be a school athletic director. She ascribes a higher status to her coaching work than to her paraeducator work or to teaching. She has some social connections with teachers in the district through coaching and her sister teaches in one of the two middle schools but she does not have the bond of living in the district or of having children attend school in the district. From her interviews and my observations of her at work, I thought that she was direct, socially adept and energetic. Assigned to a student who is oppositional to authority, she creates a role in which she self-limits her authority to reminding him of the existence of other authority.

Tiffany sorts each person she meets into categories: friend, relative or not and then builds her relationship accordingly. She treats adults she meets in her community of practice as potential extended family and children as potentially her own in a type of maternal anticipation. She looks forward to mothering her daughter and her future children the same way that she nurtures the students in her care. Like Pat, she looks forward to being a teacher but unlike Pat, she believes that as a paraeducator, she is engaged in a form of teaching. She does note the difference between her tutoring an individual or a small group and managing an entire classroom. Tiffany sees her role as analogous to a mother or to a big sister, using the framework of family structure. She expresses her agency through decisions she and the teacher make about her role in the classroom in light of the teacher's preferences and the students' needs.

Ellen describes herself as a woman with a calling to be a teacher in a spiritual sense of a mission to serve. Being a teacher is a core part of her identity. When she meets the needs of others, she is emotionally fulfilled. Like Pat and Tiffany, she aspires to be a public school classroom teacher. In her case, she would return to teaching. She recalls how she worked with a paraeducator when she was a teacher in an inner-city school and molds her own relationships with teachers according to that model. She sees herself as the teacher's "extra pair of hands". Ellen expresses her agency by framing her work as a service to others and a duty based upon a calling. She considers that her lack of agency in many of the classrooms to which she is assigned is due to lack of time within each community of practice. She believes she needs more opportunities for discourse to reveal to the teachers her capacity to do the work. Few forms of discourse were noted. If Ellen is not part of the community of practice in a number of classrooms, then her lack of forms of discourse is understandable. Indeed, the evidence of discourse in these other sites was different. There are many more directives from the teacher to the paraeducator and fewer instances of social bonding. That evidence suggests that mutual understanding between teacher and paraeducator reduces the number of directives that the teacher needs to convey during instructional time. Less time in supervision means more time that both the teacher and the paraeducator can devote to interacting with students.

Chapter 11: Measuring and Meaning

Despite many career paths, Brenda is at heart a medical worker. She monitors and nurtures the children to whom she is assigned like the patients she once had. She claims the authority she needs to perform her job based upon her personal knowledge of her student just as she based her authority as a medical technician upon her clinical knowledge of her patients. She believes in the existence of natural talent and that she has the talent needed for this job. She and Pat are the only paraeducators who did not rest their authority on experiences as parents. Pat had no children, but perhaps because Brenda had not had children until her forties, she did not ascribe her expertise to that life experience. This is a destination occupation for her, not a way station to another job. She does not aspire to be a teacher nor does she see herself as a type of teacher. She believes that her position is different from a teacher's but not less than a teacher's. She asserts that her authority supersedes a teacher's authority, but her agency is always in reaction to a teacher's or a student's actions.

Babs uses a business model and envisions her world through her understanding of group social norms. She locates her proper place in the world and urges other people, including the students with whom she works, to do the same in school. Babs sees herself as a worker. Like Brenda, she does not aspire to be a teacher and does not see herself as a type of teacher. Unlike Brenda, she does not see herself as a teacher's equal. She feels that she "fills in as needed." She is a close associate of Ellen and they share the same view of a paraeducator's place in the school hierarchy despite their very different backgrounds. They also were assigned the same type of schedule and the highest number of relationships to sustain. Like Brenda, the role she has now is the role she plans to continue in the future.

Kelsey follows a self-selected standard of conduct. She believes that she is not playing second fiddle, but helping the fiddler play. She sees herself as an assisting teacher and this occupation as her vocational and social destination. She is professional no matter what the task and she precisely measures her behavior against this internal code. Kelsey conducts herself in a manner that would be equally at home in the business world, a medical establishment, a legal office or a school. Like the other two senior paraeducators, the work she performs now is the work she plans to perform in the future. Her agency is apparent to herself as she fashions a role to meet the needs of each new assignment. She, like each of the other participants, demonstrates unique qualities, beliefs, sources of motivation and skills. Despite their individuality, the process of gaining and maintaining membership in the classroom is similar.

Evidence of Community of Practice

Using Wenger's description of a community of practice, I found evidence of a community of practice in each classroom. Through interviews and observations, I gathered instances of both the existence of a community of practice within each classroom and the participants' membership. In Ellen's case, I found evidence of a lack of membership outside of Rick Johnson's classroom. Her work, therefore, is represented by a second column on table 1 to divide her evidence in two. I did not try to quantify the number of instances for each category of evidence, but rather their existence. Some differences between paraeducators are evident on table 1. Other than Ellen, Babs has the least number of observed interactions and reported interactions. I did not have an opportunity to observe her with the teacher with whom she spends the most of her time, so the results could be skewed by that lack. Ellen's work in Rick Johnson's classroom garnered her more observed instances of interaction on Wenger's scale than outside of his classroom. Given time enough, she did join the community, albeit not as a full member.

Table 1: Community of practice membership evidence.[163]

Community of practice evidence	Pat	Tiffany	Ellen with Rick	Ellen	Brenda	Babs	Kelsey
Sustained relationships	X	X	X		X	X	X
Shared ways of doing things	X	X			X	X	X
Rapid flow of information	X	X	X		X	X	X
Absence of introductory preambles	X	X	X		X		X
Quick set-up of problem to discuss	X		X		X	X	X
Overlap in descriptions of who belongs		X					X
Knowing what others know or do	X				X		X

---

[163] Wenger, 1999.

The Paraeducator: The Other Grown-Up In The Classroom

Community of practice evidence, continued	Pat	Tiffany	Ellen with Rick	Ellen	Brenda	Babs	Kelsey
Mutually defining identities	X	X			X	X	X
Ability to assess appropriate actions	X	X	X		X	X	X
Specific tools, artifacts	X	X	X		X	X	X
Local lore, shared stories, jokes	X	X			X	X	X
Jargon and shortcuts to communicate	X	X			X		X
Certain styles display membership	X	X			X	X	X
Shared discourse reflects a certain perspective on the world	X	X				X	X
Total	13	12	6	0	12	10	14

Chapter 11: Measuring and Meaning

I observed or heard about all fourteen signs of a community of practice outlined by Wenger.[164] I saw less evidence for Ellen than for any other paraeducator, which is understandable, given her self-stated difficulty creating relationships in some of the classrooms to which she is assigned. She and the other five participants continuously work in their role in a dynamic process, evidenced by the characteristics they display as members of a community of practice. Given the existence of a community of practice, I observed and listened to evidence of how each paraeducator becomes a member.

Membership in the Community of Practice
Observation

From the paraeducators' point of view, their duties vary depending upon the needs of others. To ascertain those ever shifting needs, they need to observe the classroom. Ellen described her job with: "I go to a small group of children who need my help and then when they seem to have a handle on things, I go to another group. I know who needs help. I go around and ask the students how are you doing and if they seem to be doing okay on their own, I rotate to another table. And then, if there is ever a slow time in the class and it looks as if the children don't need my help or they are at instrument lessons, then I go to the teacher and ask if there is anything I can do."

"Well you have your antenna up, too, as you're sitting there, to see if anybody needs anything" Babs said. "I like working with Mrs. Teaberry, but it's different in social studies than it is in math. You sit and wait a lot. I like to be busy. With social studies, there is more sitting." Babs related her opinion that her role changed

---

[164] Wenger, 1999

with the subject being taught more than with the personalities of the teachers.

Pat expressed similar views: "It really depends on what we are doing that day, where my child might need more assistance, less assistance." Ellen echoed her with: "If they are doing a science experiment, Mr. Johnson would run that and I would just be there as support and assist any groups that are having trouble with it. It really depends on the subject area and what else is going on. If there's a group of kids [doing] math problems, just a small group, I may go out in the hallway with them and work out there. And that would be more of an interactive role. It really depends on what the need is at a given time."

Imagining one person in another participant's job leads to the conclusion that how each participant fulfills their role is an expression of their identity in the classroom. For example, Pat with her cautious negotiation of space would perhaps perform Brenda's role entirely differently. Each of these women formulates stories that she tells herself. These pieces of self-discourse become interpreted experience and therefore part of her identity. Each paraeducator brings this newly shaped identity to her role, and continues the cycle of identity and role development by having further discourse with the other members of the community of practice.

Communication

Communication helped them resolve ambiguities. Reiterating Ellen: "There are not a lot of things that are spelled out for us. I guess, even a lot of our responsibilities are not spelled out. We just have to look to the teacher for guidance and see what is needed at that particular period." Circumstances might change, and they adapt their behavior in reaction.

Chapter 11: Measuring and Meaning

Pat explicitly stated that she developed a good working relationship through discourse for social bonding. "In the beginning of the day, Maureen and I are both there in the classroom. We get to have personal conversations. It's not just about school. I know about her husband. Talked to her when her mom died. When you work around people you build relationships."

Tiffany also assessed her relationship with the teacher she worked with daily: "I could see us becoming friends, regardless. Cause, in the morning, we'll talk about outside stuff. My husband, her boyfriend. Just, you know, not necessarily school stuff." And the participants related that they had the same types of conversations with students. Tiffany noticed that: "They all want to tell me information all day long. I say, 'Ok, sit down and do your work. You can tell me this later.' I relate to them with different stuff...outside of school. Outside of math and English."

From observation and interview, the participants demonstrate how they create their role through communication with teachers and students. The paraeducators engaged in six different types of communication during the course of their workday. The types depended upon the purpose of what they said or the person to whom they spoke. Two of the six involved social communication for the purpose of creating or continuing social bonding with either a teacher or a student. Three were about working with the teacher, either by following a teacher's directions, clarifying what the teacher wanted her role to be through posing a question, or training through modeling. The last, solving a problem, was a series of statements engaging with either a student or a teacher.

Using consistent definitions for these interchanges, I found that five out of the six paraeducators had the same behaviors. The sixth, Ellen, did not show or report as many instances of communication during observations as did the other five paraeducators. The three areas in which she did were social bonding with either a teacher or a student and training.

Table 2: Types of communication, either observed or self-reported, by participant

Type of communication	Pat	Tiffany	Ellen	Brenda	Babs	Kelsey
Social bonding with teacher	X	X		X	X	X
Social bonding with student	X	X		X	X	X
Training	X				X	
Solving a problem	X	X	X	X	X	X
Directing a student	X	X	X	X	X	X
Following teacher directive	X	X	X	X	X	X
Clarifying role	X	X	X	X	X	X
Total	7	6	4	6	7	6

Ellen has less interaction with students and teachers than her peers.

Commitment

I cannot measure commitment, but I can enumerate the elements that may lead to a commitment to the work.

Table 3: Community of practice status variables

Variables	Pat	Tiffany	Ellen	Brenda	Babs	Kelsey
Prior work	X	X	X	X	X	X
Paraeducator elsewhere			X		X	X
Experience at site				X	X	X
Teaching certificate			X			X
Sponsor	X	X		X	X	X
Staff social connections	X	X				X
Lives in district			X	X		X
Children		X	X	X	X	X
Child attends school district			X	X		X
College degree	X	X	X	X		X
Other role	X*					
Does not photocopy	X	X		X		X
Does not do lunch duty				X	X	X
Total	6	6	7	9	6	12

*coach

Low status markers are photocopying and outside lunch duty/recess, according to senior participants. The principal does not assign outside lunch duty/recess to experienced paraeducators but does routinely assign the novices. Teachers assign photocopying according to where they think the paraeducator will be most useful: either making copies or working within the classroom. That reasoning encapsulates the low status for photocopying.

I considered assigning a weight to some markers. For example, having a sponsor seems to be worth more than many other status markers. A sponsor would be able to inform the participant about the important members in the community of practice, what they could accomplish, how to problem solve and many other pieces of information about people and processes that are known to insiders. A sponsor gave entry and supported continued membership. Some sponsors, such as Tiffany's and Pat's, were part of the paraeducators' everyday life either at home or at school.

Another marker that carried more weight than many others was time employed as a paraeducator in this particular school. The importance of this marker seems to fit in with how people gain and sustain membership in a community of practice. Time in this school would give other members of the community of practice opportunity to know a paraeducator's training, background and talents. Ellen mentioned this factor in her note to me. Time in the school would give the paraeducator opportunities to both make social connections and learn the habits and practices within one or more communities of practice.

Looking at the total number of plus markers minus negative markers, Brenda and Kelsey are three and six points higher than the other four paraeducators. Given their time in the system, these higher scores are not surprising. On the surface, Babs' lower score is unexpected. Her background may explain her score. She is the only participant without a year of college and trained through an in-district alternate route. Lack of teacher training might limit her capacity for the work when compared to that of her better-trained peers.

High status enables a quick entry into the community and reflects the level of potential status. These markers did not, however, predict how the individuals interpret the role. Under these broadly illustrated individual descriptions lie common approaches to fulfilling job expectations, but not common results.

The participants created their role with their identity and thus, their capacity within the confines of the context.

Adaptor

Even when developed, they did not see their role as set or immutable. Babs advised: "What the teachers need is different from period to period and from day to day. And the students are different from period to period and day to day at times." Many factors that influence their job are outside their control. Teachers go on maternity leave, children move and administrators change their schedules. They expected to develop their role based upon their capacity, the teacher's preferences and the students' needs. The participants expected this development to be on going, in order to prevent role confusion.

This finding supports the conclusions of previous researchers who found role confusion endemic because these paraeducators constantly work to prevent that confusion and adapt to changing circumstances through the relationships they develop during their time in the community of practice. The strength and the weakness of this occupation are two sides of the same coin. Adaptation means that change is constant and in response to current needs.

Partner

Each paraeducator anticipated temporary role confusion at the beginning of the school year, until she and the teacher and students established a working relationship. For example, they worked out their roles for discipline within the classroom early in the year. Tiffany said: "And in the beginning, Cindy said: 'Let me be the dragon lady. I'll be the one. I'll fuss at them and stuff.'" Kelsey and her teacher reached the opposite arrangement; Kelsey was the disciplinarian. In some cases, especially if they only worked together for one forty-minute period during the week, their relationship was more difficult to establish. Tiffany explained:

"The other teachers, since I'm not as close to them, I don't say: 'Maybe we should do that.' But I tell them: 'If you want me to discipline her, I will step in.'" The point was not that there was a set way to divide the work, but that the people involved agreed on how to divide the work.

In addition, many saw themselves engaged in a social job. "Getting along" and "liking" were words that Babs used to describe her relationships with teachers and students. She acknowledged the children with a Valentine's Day card and they reciprocated with verbal thanks and physical hugs. Kelsey said bluntly: "The nature of the job calls for being social. It's not the type of job a person can do who is not social."

But the process hinges upon a variable that is largely out of the paraeducators' control—time.

Time Spent in the Community of Practice

These processes are dependent upon the amount of time each paraeducator would have in each community of practice. Time is the fulcrum that allows them to behave socially and create their membership.

Ellen found it difficult to find the time and opportunity to have the type of talk that clarified ambiguity when she had a conflict. While Ellen asserted that she implicitly understood the purpose of school and "how to be in a classroom," she also said that she needed to know how to be in each particular classroom. "It is hard for me to keep up with what the class is doing when you know I am not with them on a daily basis. But there are some teachers I am with every day and things go a little smoother when they know me and I know them." Tiffany echoed the same thought, but had ample time with one teacher: "Well, we've been in a classroom with each other since September, that's almost six months. Cause it's the same stuff every day, every day. Kids do the same things every day. So we know what's going on." Tiffany concluded: "We talk. We talk a lot." Several participants reported that they were careful not to encroach on the teachers' territory. Potential role confusion was sometimes handled in the moment: "I will ask before I go ahead and take over something" Pat said." Tiffany expressed the same view: "But me being the aide, I tell myself this is her class (the teacher's), and I'm here to help. I will ask her: 'Do you need help, do you need me to grade papers, blah, blah, this and that?' And I help her out."

They received clarifications on their behavior in the classroom. Babs described how teachers had told her what she needed to do during her first year of work. "The teachers helped me to figure the job out and then, I could help them."

Ellen serves as a negative example to prove the point that role confusion can be dispelled through adequate time in the community of practice. Ellen has more formal educational training than any other participant. She has a master's degree in reading, and yet of all the participants, she expressed the most difficulty in her job during the course of the study. Given Ellen's educational background, her lack of formal training cannot be the factor that causes her difficulty. She had the most fragmented schedule of all the paraeducators, with the greatest number of classes in which she appeared once per week (table 5) and the greatest number of students for whom she was responsible (table 6). She had twenty-seven students among eight classes, taught by nine teachers. Even if she never talked to any member of her classes other than the teachers and her assigned students, she would have thirty-eight relationships to develop. She talked about a "lack of time" for forging relationships.

The Paraeducator: The Other Grown-Up In The Classroom

The other paraeducators had many less. Two of the paraeducators had seven relationships to nurture; one had nine and another, eleven. Thus, Ellen had less time to take part in the two types of classroom discourse that, from observation and interviews, would help her forge a place in each community of practice: clarification discourse and bonding discourse. Her only recourse would be to voluntarily extend her workday, either before or after school, to spend time with the teachers. Even if she had come to work early and stayed late, she worked with too many teachers to make social connections on a daily basis feasible. In addition, she had undertaken this job to be more available for her family than she would be if she worked as a teacher. Extending her hours would have undermined her own personal goals. As a result, she was a visitor to many of the classrooms rather than a participant in their communities of practice. The impact on her identity was negative. She felt that the teachers did not see her as an equal and she looked to them as her supervisors. She longed to be a teacher again "where I could be in a classroom all day."

Her flexibility within this imposed restriction was minimal. Her formal training, while helpful, was not the only factor she needed for success in the role. The schedule was not by her choice, but created by administrators to meet the legal definition of, if not the spirit of, paraeducator support written into students' Individualized Educational Plans. The school administrators created work schedules that held the same amount of work hours, but the number of relationships each paraeducator maintains is unequal.

Quantifying Workload via Social Relationships

The difficulty of a child, the receptiveness of a teacher, or the chemistry of a classroom of children is hard to quantify, but I can compute the number of relationships each paraeducator needs to sustain. For example, in table 4, Pat, Tiffany and Kelsey have the fewest number of teacher relationships while Ellen and Babs have the most, with a range of 5 to 9 with five being the least and nine being the most.

Table 4 Periods per week paraeducator is with teacher.

Teacher:	A	B	C	D	E	F	G	H	I
Participant									
Pat	15	5	5	2	1	1	1		
Tiffany	25	2	1	1	1				
Ellen	14	5	4	2	1	1	1	1	1
Brenda	12	10	5	4	2	1	1		
Babs	14	5	5	4	2	2	1	1	1
Kelsey	25	2	1	1	1				

Table 5 Weekly number of teachers with each paraeducator.

Participant	Total # of Teachers
Pat	7
Tiffany	5
Ellen	9
Brenda	7
Babs	9
Kelsey	5

Babs and Ellen have 80% more "relationship load" with teachers than do Kelsey, Tiffany and Pat. Ellen has only two teachers she works with on a daily basis and seven with whom she works with less frequently. Brenda and Pat have three academic teachers they work with daily and four teachers they see less often.

The paraeducator has student relationships to maintain by assignment. Each group of students forms another community of practice, even if the students share teachers when they rotate between teachers for science, math and/or social studies.

Table 5 represents the number of forty-minute periods each participant spends in each classroom to which they are assigned.

Table 6 Number of periods paraeducator is with each group of students weekly.

Participant	Group A	B	C	D	E	F	G
Pat	35*						
Tiffany	35*						
Ellen	14	10 *	6	1	1	1	1
Brenda	20	10	5				
Babs	21	5	5	2	1		
Kelsey	35*						

*lunch coverage has no teacher present

Table 7 Number of different groups of students paraeducator is with each week.

Participant	Groups
Pat	1
Tiffany	1
Ellen	7
Brenda	3
Babs	5
Kelsey	1

Again, there is a range. Pat, Kelsey and Tiffany are with one group of students all day long. Brenda's student joins three different groups of classmates throughout the day. Babs spends the majority of her week, over 60% of her time, with one class. Ellen, in contrast, spends 40% of her week with Rick Johnson's students, 29% of her week with Leslie Stands' students, 17% with a third group and has 4 classes of students with whom she spends 3.3% of her work week. Ellen says that she feels a connection with Rick's class, but not with any other class. Her ten-period a week assignment is actually a class period and a lunch period spent with a small subset of the children from the class. And then there are four classes of students she sees for one period per week.

Within these classroom groups of students, paraeducators are directly assigned to a number of students. Although they may interact with other students in the periphery, they are assigned to focus on certain students. The number of targeted students varies with each paraeducator, as illustrated in Table 6.

Table 8 Number of students for whom each paraeducator has direct responsibility in each class in which they work

Participants	Class A	B	C	D	E	F	G	H	Total # students
Pat	1								1
Tiffany	1								1
Ellen	4	1	6	1	6	1	1	6	26
Brenda	1								1
Babs	6	1	4	3	6				20
Kelsey	1								1

I do not attempt to measure the difficulty of each student. If I did, Pat and Brenda would have a weighted score. Both of their students required a high level of attention. If I take the number of relationships each participant was expected to maintain, using teachers, targeted students and classrooms as units, I can crudely quantify each participant's workload.

Table 9 Participants' workload via social relationships, with a value of one for each total column from number of teachers (table 5), groups of students(table 7) and targeted students (table 8).

Participants	Total
Pat	9
Tiffany	7
Ellen	42
Brenda	11
Babs	34

Ignoring the relative difficulty of each relationship for the sake of discussion, for surely Brenda's targeted student required more attending than many of Ellen's, Ellen has a greater social load than any other participant. Babs, despite her seniority, comes in the closest to Ellen. The more classrooms a paraeducator is assigned too, the more relationships she has to sustain while the less time she has to develop them.

Despite Ellen's teacher training, she finds her job very difficult. Perhaps she does not have the tools for successful fulfillment of her role and the tool she needs is beyond her control. Babs, on the other hand, with a heavy social load, expects nothing different and accepted the job as it was. Babs has little background training or experience in classrooms prior to her employment as a paraeducator. This observation leads to a consideration of role.

Role

The third research question concerned the paraeducators understanding of their role. The participants said that they either expected to help the teacher teach, help the students learn, or to do a combination of the two. Pat did both. She knew that she had a "policewoman" function with Jack to keep the peace so that the teachers and the other students could fulfill their role expectations. She also saw herself as "Maureen's policewoman" when she enforced the teacher's rules. She coached, prompted and exhorted Jack to fulfill his role as a student. Despite that focus, she was clear that she reports to and is supervised by the teachers.

Pat saw herself in a more family-member relationship with the other students. "I am the liaison between the teacher and the student. I sit at a lunch table with some of the girls. I find out before she does. I'm the sister-in-the-family kind of thing." She saw her rank in the community of practice as below a teacher and above a student, and serves as a bridge between the two.

Tiffany's priority was also to the teacher as the person responsible for the entire classroom. She assisted the teacher by performing duties the teacher would normally have done herself that were not directly instructional. For example, Tiffany chopped onions for the science lab experiment and collected books at the end of a Shakespeare lesson. Tiffany tutored the students and individually clarified questions that they had about assignments and grades. Tiffany felt that the general education teacher confirmed her status: "And a couple of times, Miss Sharp said like: 'She is a teacher, you have to listen to her.'" Tiffany saw her relationship to the teacher as an assisting teacher, who also served as a tutor for an individual or a group, saying: "I never get up in front of the class, presenting a lecture. Miss Sharp may say something, and I may add on to something she may say. But it's more a tutor than a teacher, than actually teaching a whole group." Tiffany saw herself as in a narrower role, not because of lack of authority, but because of lack of responsibility for the entire classroom. She did imply that sense of being in-between the students when she talked about being "a big sister" and, in a type of maternal anticipation, regarded the students as examples of how her own possible future children would behave at that age.

Ellen envisions herself as "an extra pair of hands" for the teachers and for one of her students, she is "her right hand". Ellen's fragmented schedule seems to make her less able to help teachers because she did not know the classroom routine or the teachers' plans for the day. During my observations, she spent most of her time directly assisting students, either through small-group instruction or on a one-to-one basis. Sometimes, she assisted students when her help seemed unneeded to keep herself looking engaged in classrooms where she lacked membership.

Brenda is very clear that her job is to help her student learn. When she feels that she is treated as a colleague, she is happy to help a teacher. The type of help that one teacher wants she believes is denigrating work fit for a servant and she will not help her. Brenda sees herself as a teacher's equal and sometimes a superior. "I think of myself as not an assistant, because I am not really assisting them. I am the expert on the child."

Babs, although a senior paraeducator by virtue of her time in the school, has the same view as Ellen. Babs envisions herself as a substitute for a teacher, but not a teacher's equal. She declares that she is an "extra pair of hands" for the teachers, which incidentally includes supporting the students.

Kelsey is equally clear in her understanding of the job, although her view differs from Babs'. She is an assisting teacher who helps children learn. The divide between assisting the teacher and assisting the student deserves a close inspection. This divide is not as large as it may seem on the surface, because paraeducators are not charged with doing the teaching and learning themselves. They are enjoined to help the student learn, which is itself another way of saying "teaching". The distinction may be more one of competing needs rather than competing tasks.

The answers to one of the core research questions of this study depend upon the definition of role confusion. Many researchers describe role confusion as a chronic disorganized state. These paraeducators see it as a fluid state that they negotiate and clarify as they had time in the classroom with the teacher and students. Given the right circumstances, confusion was temporary once they set up working relationships. In this light, confusion is a positive because the job is not done by repetition and rote. Through resolving confusion, paraeducators tailor their support to meet individual needs.

In one rare case that proves the rule, time did not help. Kelsey, Brenda, and Tiffany alluded to difficulty working with the same teacher, Leslie Stands. What makes Leslie hard to work with is her refusal to do the things that members of a community of practice expect of each other. "And we know that there are people here, that when the IA is in the room, they don't even want them to talk. You don't say anything, you are not to be heard, you just sit there until they need you," said Brenda. Lack of talk was tantamount to lack of a way to create a relationship and lack of a way to perform their job.

Creating a good working relationship is not, therefore, always within their control. Their agency is limited and confined by the context of their role. A paraeducator has an internal locus of control only in her reactions to the environment. Her job is crucially different from the teacher's position. The teacher is the dominant person in the classroom while the paraeducator is expected to assist others in the community of practice. With her dependency upon the teacher, she is more akin to the students. In this halfway land, she navigates between childlike dependency and adult agency. The adolescent "older sister" imagery was invoked by both Pat and Tiffany to describe this in-between state.

From the examples of these participants, the paraeducator is a person who observes the community of practice she is to join, and in reaction adapts her role as a paraeducator through communication. Each position varies one from the other and sometimes varies from one moment to the next, which evidences the adaptive nature of their occupation. If the defining difference between a paraeducator and a teacher is agency, than a different set of skills is important, and informal training within the community of practice is a crucial factor in their success.

If paraeducators are teachers-in-waiting, or junior teachers or substitutes for teachers, then teacher training is needed. If paraeducators are engaged in a separate occupation, which overlaps with the occupation of teaching, then they may need additional and somewhat different training to prepare them for and sustain them in their occupation.

Training

All six paraeducators affirm that they have an innate ability or predisposition for the work. Pat, Babs and Kelsey cited their social skills, Brenda her ability to read people's feelings and Ellen a calling to teach. The participants cite four different ways they learned to become the other grown-up in the classroom: a predisposition for the work, formal teacher training, and training on the job through imitating teachers and direct instruction from teachers. Tiffany, Ellen and Kelsey learned how to perform their job through college education coursework. Ellen, Kelsey, Tiffany and Pat attribute learning how to be a paraeducator to their experiences of being a teacher in the past. Pat and Babs say they learned to do the job from on the job training given to them by the teachers with whom they work.

According to several theorists, if paraeducators were trained, they would know what to do and be more helpful to teachers and students. This assumption underlies many of the studies in the review of the literature.[165] Training in the literature is defined implicitly as formal academic study.

Ellen and Kelsey echoed the researchers views. Ellen said succinctly: "My education background, I mean, I know how to be in the classroom." Other paraeducators felt they had training, albeit gained outside of a college classroom. Babs feels: "Well, some of it is mother instinct or dealing with people, because I dealt with people as a secretary. I have been dealing with people. It's people skills, mostly. I had four children and read a lot of books when I was raising them. You know, I threw some of it out, cause it made no sense, but I did read Dr. Spock."[166] Each paraeducator recalled valuable training experiences prior to starting the school year.

Despite that training, they talked about a period of time in the beginning of a new assignment in which they worked toward understanding what they should do in the classroom. Kelsey talked about the need to observe and draw conclusions before starting to interact with the members of the classroom, acknowledging the

---

[165] Chopra et al, 2004; Downing, 2000; French, 2004; Giangreco, 1999, Hughes, 1993; Milner, 1998

[166] Dr. Benjamin Spock, childrearing expert of the 1950's, 60's and 70's.

classrooms as idiosyncratic. Ellen needed to supplement her knowledge gained through formal training of how to be in a classroom with informal training to learn how to be in a particular classroom. While the paraeducators did not have textbooks or written exams, they were learning and getting feedback from teachers about their performance.

Training, like the role itself, has a wide range of possibilities and forms. Time in the community of practice allows them to communicate with other members and try out behaviors, which is a form of training. If training is defined as time in the classroom and discourse with teachers and students, then the paraeducators echo the need for training found in the literature.

Results

Much of what paraeducators do they come equipped to perform, through understanding and life experiences with social behaviors. The results of this study do not negate the need for training, but suggest that time in the community of practice building relationships, modeling teachers' behavior and receiving direct guidance from teachers constitutes a valuable form of training. Ellen noted the need for time to develop relationships with teachers: "When you are coming in and the kids are already there, there is no time to discuss anything. Last year, the teacher that I worked with was a little more up front about when she had workshop. She'd say: 'I won't be in tomorrow morning.' But not all teachers are like that." She then considered a factor other than the teacher's personality: "But I was with her all day, too. It's a little different when you are with someone all day as opposed to just one, two or three periods a day."

Brenda explained the importance of time to develop relationships with students: "And I talk a lot to the other kids in the classroom. They say, because I am the other adult in the classroom, the ones that are really comfortable with me will come and say things to me that they may not to the teacher. It's not that they wouldn't trust or go to Rachelle or to Susan Compton, but they see me all the time and they see how I work with Martin. If I were mean or nasty with Martin, they would back off. But if they see me as a comforting person, someone you can trust, they come to me a lot: 'Mrs. Carlsen, can I do this? Mrs. Carlsen, did you see this?' "

Training via formal instruction and developing membership in a community of practice are two very different activities. Researchers, administrators and teachers who have agency can see training via college courses or in-service workshops as concrete items in their figured world. These same people, such as myself, that is, researchers who are often college professors and administrators who are former classroom teachers, are comfortable and conversant with providing formal training. Training is usually discussed as a discrete event, which has a beginning, middle and an end. Entering and sustaining membership in a community of practice, however, is a process for training that is more difficult to visualize and not static. Membership in a community of practice is something everyone has within the system, but which is less apparent because it is ongoing, all the time. Like the air that surrounds us, it is transparent and present, noticed only when poor in quality or absent.

Chapter Twelve
Conclusions And Implications

Paraeducators are assigned to classrooms where their presence signals an implicit, presumed lack of competence in the learners' learning. Such a negative premise for their presence requires them to carefully negotiate their entry and continued membership in the classroom community.

The results further suggest that background training, work experience, innate talent for the occupation and teaching experience, while important, are not a substitute for time in the community of practice. Paraeducator participants reported, and I observed, that they use that time to build social relationships that enabled them to perform their job and make on-going adjustments in the role as needed. The phrase "as needed" underscores their use of social judgment to determine the appropriate timing and type of help. "As needed" presumes an understanding of the social, academic and behavioral norms of the community of practice.

Analysis of these conversations and observations attest that these paraeducators work in a role that contains multiple possibilities and thus, is fraught with inherent tension. All participants reported instances of stress and tension due to the ambiguity of the range of possible job demands. The mundane chore of photocopying serves as an example of this potential tension through possibilities. Brenda adamantly refused to photocopy; Kelsey noted that she did not do as much photocopying as she had when she first began work as a paraeducator; Babs was told by the principal to do less photocopying while Pat and Ellen photocopied frequently; Tiffany never even mentioned photocopying as part of her work. The parameters of each job varied, thus showing the wide range of possible demands and possible responses to those demands in their role.

Each paraeducator came to their occupation with their own personality and goals for their work. Their interpretation of the demands of the job and their view of the job is the lens through which they viewed the community of practice of each classroom they entered. The results of this research, from observations and interviews, show that paraeducators adapt to many shifting needs. Therein rests both their importance and the potential for confused role boundaries.

Studying these particular paraeducators holds importance because in this time and place, they demonstrate an ideal practice of their occupation. They are not marginalized by gender, race or socio-economic status, as found in many other studies. A researcher noted that paraeducators "tend to be of low socioeconomic status"[167] while another stated that good paraeducators are difficult to hire and to retain[168] and a third reports that they are often members of minority, underrepresented groups .[169] In contrast to what published studies have revealed, the paraeducators in the East Brighton-Fieldtown district are not all members of minority, underrepresented groups. They are not of low socio-economic status. They seem to be relatively easy to hire to work in the Water Wheel School because as one or two positions come open each year, according to the principal, she has a choice of several candidates competing for each one.[170] Many of the paraeducators stay in the job for many years. The school

---

[167] Bernal and Aragon, 2004
[168] Giangreco et al, 2005
[169] SPeNSE, 2001
[170] Abrams, private conversation, 2006

environment is not the norm due to its orderly students, supportive parents, engaged teachers and administrators and abundant resources.

This discrepancy between paraeducators found in the research literature and participants at the Water Wheel School suggests that they have differing experiences due to differing circumstances. The divergence of this ideal setting from the norm may limit the generalizability of the results of this study to other settings. Despite that caution, elements of the research hold suggestions for practice and future research.

The findings in this study are cogent for personnel practices in recruitment, hiring, work assignment and retention. In the Water Wheel School, five out of six paraeducators reported being recruited by members of the community of practice. By recommending them for employment, these sponsors implicitly vouched for their compatible skills and shared understandings. They served as bridges between the job-candidate paraeducators and the school district. Meltzoff, a social learning psychologist, says that mentors can change the social status of those they mentor.[171] Results of this study suggest that pairing each newly hired or newly assigned paraeducator with a member of the staff might replicate the benefits of the informal sponsor relationships reported by the participants: quicker entry into the community of practice and on-going support to maintain that membership.

This informal arrangement may be difficult to establish as a formal support in a large urban setting where community cohesiveness is diffuse and the school hierarchy is complex. In large school districts, the administrator who hires paraeducators may be far removed from the location in which they are to work.

---

[171] 2009

Despite that remove, interviewers could discuss the social demands of the role with candidates.

In practice, members of the school administration tacitly acknowledge the range of the position and do not place paraeducators in positions haphazardly. Often, principals or supervisors of special education consider what they know about the individual paraeducator's capacities and place her accordingly. Based upon the results of this study, administrators would be able to make better placement decisions by equitably distributing the workload via quantifying the number of social relationships and the assigned time (or lack thereof) in each community of practice.

Time in each classroom is the variable beyond training, beyond the control of the individual paraeducator.[172] In the process of gaining and sustaining membership in the community of practice, paraeducators can clarify the boundaries of their work.

Beyond time in the community of practice, the research results suggest that social behavior awareness training would support paraeducators' practice. I am deliberately avoiding the use of the phrase "social skills", which for special education practitioners resonates with overtones of deficit and training of children on the autism spectrum. Explicit discussion of implicit behaviors, behaviors that they have, such as when Pat introduced herself to a newly hired lunchroom aide, would be a valuable part of in-service training.

Facts and rules are not as helpful as boundaries and principles in an occupation that is social in nature. Content lectures should incorporate face-to-face discussions of how to apply those principles to types of teachers, classes, students and circumstances, preferably in a format that allows novices to confer with seasoned

---

[172] In a time of financial strains, their time in the classroom may be beyond the control of many administrators.

paraeducators. The lens of developing membership in a community of practice encompasses both training paraeducators to work in classrooms and training teachers to supervise paraeducators. Mutual, side-by-side, in the same room training can focus on the teacher and the paraeducator building a relationship. In this study, the social bond between teachers and paraeducators shortens the distance between ranks of the school hierarchy, secures trust, mutual respect and ultimately, gains time for teaching students.

Through the process of developing membership in the community of practice, one participant, Pat, changed from a novice to an experienced member during the six months course of my study. Tiffany stayed engaged, somewhere in-between a novice and an experienced member of the community of practice. Three participants present themselves as having, and I observed them to exhibit, seasoned and stable membership in the community over the six months of the study. Lacking membership, Ellen is blocked from discourse and remained a novice in several classrooms throughout the year. Further research in other sites using a social lens is needed.

As part of the reform of special education, the paraeducators' job mirrors the purpose of special education to broaden the range of children who attend general education classes. This job is essentially conservative in nature as is special education. Special education is designed to uphold the status quo not to reform or radicalize general education. General education is tacitly understood to be desirable. Paraeducators are recruited and seen as potential members in the community of practice because they demonstrate agreement with community norms. Norms by definition are the antithesis of radical changes and reforms. The reformers of special education did not foresee the rise of this occupation nor its nature. The reformers also did not foresee the gendered nature of the occupation.

The suspicion that paraeducators are engaging in a gendered occupation is the eight hundred and fifty pound gorilla that future research may fruitfully drag into the discussion of their occupation. Many of the attributes and demands of the role are those closely associated with behavior linked to female gender archetypes: an ethic of caring, social responsiveness, subordination, care of the young, preservation of cultural mores and valuing social relationships. The paraeducators in this book are female, as are most of the teachers for whom they work, the child study team members, the principal and vice-principal and the superintendent. Being female is the gender that is the norm, the default gender. In a different setting, being female and in this role may have a negative connotation. The identity and role they construct is not that of hero or anti-hero, but is the perennial supportive role based upon cooperative work. Since paraeducators construct the meaning of their work socially through face-to-face interaction then further research into how they engage socially may contribute to the small extant body of research. With only seven studies on paraeducators published between 1999 and 2006, researchers have many gaps in the literature to fill.[173]

The paraeducators work at the messy edges of school practice. The division between a layperson with innate talent and a professional with more formal credentials may be an inherent distinction between paraeducators and teachers. Of course, having ability and training is the ideal for both positions. The flexibility of the position suggests a need for a careful match of a paraeducator's talents to student needs as well as training. A fuller understanding

---

[173] Nevin, Malian and Liston, 2008

of the relationships between them and students and teachers may be particularly critical at a time when schools and paraeducators are facing new requirements and the pressure of imposed change.

Communicating with and about paraeducators is important to teachers and students and the paraeducators themselves because although the word "teacher" is rarely applied to paraeducators in the research literature, paraeducators *do* instruct, support, assist, tutor, and reinforce the learning of students who have academic, social and emotional difficulties.

I hope this book prompts further research into the identity, role and relationships of the other grown-up in the classroom as well as changes in practices of hiring, scheduling and training paraeducators. The members of this occupation deserve recognition for the negotiation and performance of their complex work.

References

The Fourteenth Amendment (1888).

H.R. 1350, Individuals with Disabilities Education Amendments Act (IDEA) (1997).

Public Law 105-17, Individuals with Disabilities Education Improvement Act (IDEIA) (2004).

Public Law 94-142 Education for All Handicapped Children Act (1975).

Brown vs. the Board of Education, 347 U.S. 483 (1954).

Mills v. Board of Education. (DC District Court 1972).

Pennsylvania Association for Retarded Children v. Pennsylvania, (United States 3rd district 1971).

Anderson, Gary L, Herr, Kathryn, Nihlen, Ann Sigrid (1994). *Studying Your Own School.* Thousand Oaks, CA: Corwin Press, Sage Publications.

Bernal, C. & Aragon, Lorenso (2004). Critical Factors Affecting the Success of Paraprofessionals in the First Two Years of Career Ladder Projects in Colorado. *Remedial and Special Education 25(4):* 205+.

Blair, Roger & Sailor, Wayne (2005). Rethinking Inclusion: Schoolwide Applications. *Phi Delta Kappan.* 86 (7). 503+.

Borden, D. B. a. M. (2004). Special Education History Parallels Civil Rights Movement. *Down Syndrome Association of Orange County.*

Bowles, Samuel and Gintis, Herbert. (1975). Capitalism and Education in the United States. *Socialist Revolution*, 5.

Broer, S, Doyle, M. & Giangreco, M. (2005). Perspectives of Students with Intellectual Disabilities about Their Experiences with Paraprofessional Support. *Exceptional Children* 71(4): 415+.

Carroll, Diane. (2001). Considering Paraprofessional Training, Roles and Responsibilities. *Teaching Exceptional Children*, 34 (2) 60-64.

Chopra, R., Sandoval-Lucero, E., Aragon, L., Bernal, C., Berg De Balderas, H., & Carroll, D. (2004). The Paraprofessional Role of Connector. *Remedial and Special Education 25(4):* 219+.

Clandinin, Jean, D. ed. *Handbook of Narrative Inquiry.* Thousand Oaks: SAGE Publications, 2007.

Cohen, Arie and Daniels, Victor. (2001). Responses to "Empirical and Hermeneutic Approaches to Phenomenological Research in Psychology, A Comparison." *Gestalt! 5*(2). Retrieved November 20, 2002 from http://www.g-g.org/gej/

Connell, R. W. (2002). *Gender.* Cambridge: Polity Press.

Cremin, Lawrence. (1961). *The Transformation of the School.* New York: Vintage Books, Random House.

References

Creswell, John W. (1998). *Qualitative Inquiry and Research Design*. Thousand Oaks, CA, Sage.

Cuban, L. (1993). *How Teachers Taught: Constancy and Change in American Classrooms 1880-1990*. New York and London, Teachers College Press.

Cuban, L. (1998). How Schools Change Reforms: Redefining Reform Success and Failure. *Teachers College Record* Volume 99 Number 3, 1998, p.453-477 http://www.tcrecord.org ID Number: 10273, Date Accessed: 2/9/2007 3:40:37PM

Downing, June E., Ryndak, Diane L. & Clark, Denise. (2000). Paraprofessionals in Inclusive Classrooms, Their Own Perceptions. *Remedial and Special Education*, 21 (3) 171-181.

Erikson, E.H. (1968). *Identity: Youth and crisis*. New York: Norton.

Emerson, Robert M., Fretz, Rachel I., & Shaw, Linda L. (1995). *Writing Ethnographic Fieldnotes*. Chicago and London: The University of Chicago Press.

Fitch, Frank. (2003). Inclusion, Exclusion, and Ideology: Special Education Students' Changing Sense of Self. *The Urban Review (35)* 3, 233-252.

Franklin, B. M. (1994). From "Backwardness" to "At-Risk": Childhood Learning Difficulties and the Contradictions of School Reform. Albany, New York, State University of New York Press.

French, Nancy K. (2001). Supervising Paraprofessionals: A Survey of Teacher Practices. *Journal of Special Education* 34: 1-23.

French, Nancy K. (2004). Paraprofessional Relationships with Parents of Students with Significant Disabilities. *Remedial and Special Education* 25 (4):240+.

Gee, James P., Hull, G. and Lankshear, C. (1996). The New Work Order: Behind the Language of the New Capitalism. Boulder, CO: Westview Press.

Giangreco, M.F., Edelman, S. W., and Broer, S.M. (1999). The Tip of the Iceberg: Determining whether paraprofessional support is needed for students with disabilities in general education settings. *The Journal of the Association of Persons with Severe Handicaps, 24*:280-290

Giangreco, M., Broer, & Edelman, S. (2001). Respect, Acknowledgement and Appreciation of Paraprofessionals Who Support Students with Disabilities. *Exceptional Children* 67(4):485-498

Giangreco, M., Edelman, S. & Broer, S. (2003). Schoolwide Planning to Improve Paraprofessional Supports. *Exceptional Children* 70(1): 63+.

Giangreco, M., Broer, & Edelman, S. (2005). "Be Careful What You Wish for...": Five Reasons to Be concerned About the Assignment of Individual Paraprofesisonalss.

References

Giangreco, M., Edelman, S., Broer, S& Doyle, Mary Beth (2001). Paraprofessional Support of Students with Disabilities: Literature from the Past Decade. *Exceptional Children 68(1)*: 45.

Giroux, H. A. (1997). *Pedagogy and the Politics of Hope: Theory, Culture, and Schooling: A Critical Reader.* Boulder, CO: Westview Press.

Glaser, Barney G. and Strauss, Anselm L. (1967). *The Discovery of Grounded Theory: Strategies for Qualitative Research.* Aldine de Gruyter, New York.

Gredler, Margaret E. and Green, Susan K. (2002). A Review and Analysis of Constructivism for School-Based Practice. *School Psychology Review*, 31 (1).

Hall, L.J., McClannahan, L.E., and Krantz, P.J. (1995). Promoting independence in integrated classrooms by teaching aides to use activity schedules and decreased prompts. *Education and Training in Mental Retardation and Developmental Disabilities, 30*, 208-217.

Hein, Serge and Austin, Wendy. (2001). Empirical and Hermeneutic Approaches to Phenomenological Research in Psychology, A Comparison. *Psychological Methods, 6* (1) 3-17.

Holland, Dorothy, Lachicotte, W., Skinner, D,.Cain, Carole (1998) *Identity and Agency in Cultural Worlds* Cambridge, Mass: Harvard University Press.

Hughes, R. J. (1993). Beyond the Expert Helping Model. *Journal of Extension 31 (1).*

Juzwik, Mary M. (2006) Situating Narrative-Minded Research: A Commentary on Anna Sfard and Anna Prusak's "Telling Identities". *Educational Researcher, 35* (9) 13-21.

Kvale, Steinar (1996). *InterViews.* Thousand Oaks, CA: Sage.

Labaree, David F. (1997) *How to Succeed in School Without Really Learning.* New Haven and London: Yale University Press.

Lave, Jean and Wenger, Etienne. (1991) *Situated Learning: Legitimate Peripheral Participation.* Cambridge, England: Cambridge University Press.

Lewis, Karla C. (2003) *Colleagues or Cultural Brokers? Instructional Aides; Relationships with Teachers and Parents.* Paper presented at the Annual Meeting of the American Educational Research Association, Chicago, Ill.

Lortie, Dan C. (1975). *Schoolteacher.* Chicago and London: The University of Chicago Press.

Levine, M. S. U. M., Carl Schrader (1999). Paraeducator Experiences in Inclusive Settings: Helping, Hovering or Holding Their Own? *Exceptional Children 65(3):* 315.

Marshall, Catherine and Rossman, Gretchen B. (1999). *Designing Qualitative Research.* (3rd ed.). Thousand Oaks, CA: Sage.

References

Marshall, Gordon (1994). *Dictionary of Sociology.* (2nd ed.). Oxford, England: Oxford University Press.

Martell, R.C., Marchaud-Martella, N.E.,Miller, T. L., Young, K.R., and MacFarlane, C.A. (1995). Teaching instructional aides and peer tutors to decrease problem behaviors in the classroom. *Teaching Exceptional Children, 27*(2), 53-56.

Martin, Edwin R. M. a. D. T. (1996). The Legislative and Litigation History of Special Education. *The Future of Children* 6(1): 25-39.

Mclaughlin, Margaret J. & Warren, Sandra H. (1994). The Costs of Inclusion. *School Administrator, (51)* 10: 8+.

Meltzoff, Andrew. (2009) From baby scientist to a science of social learning. *Science News.* 176 (7):32.

Merriam, Sharan. (1998). Case study research in education: A qualitative approach (2nd ed.). San Francisco: Jossey-Bass.

Milner, C.A. (1998). Paraprofessional in Inclusive Classrooms: Working without a Net. Doctoral dissertation, The University of North Dakota. *Dissertation Abstract International, 59,* 1527.

Morgan-Fleming, Riegle and Fryer, "Narrative Inquiry in Archival Work", in Sharan B. Merriam and Associates, *Qualitative Research in Practice.* San Francisco: Jossey-Bass, 2002.

Murphy, P. (ed.) (1999) *Learners, Learning and Assessment,* London: Paul Chapman. See, also, Leach, J. and Moon, B. (eds.) (1999) *Learners and Pedagogy,* London: Paul

Chapman. 280 + viii pages; and McCormick, R. and Paetcher, C. (eds.) (1999) *Learning and Knowledge,* London: Paul Chapman. 254 + xiv pages.

Nevin, A., Malian, I., and Liston, A. (2008). *Paraprofessional's Profile in Inclusive Classrooms: Analysis of National Survey Data and Follow-up Case Study Interviews in California.* Paper presented at Nation Resource Center for Paraeducators 27th National Conference on the Training and Employment of Paraeducators in Hartford, CT.

Patton, M.Q. (1990). *Qualitative Research and Evaluation Methods.* Beverly Hills, CA: Sage.

Reich, Warren A. (2000). Identity Structure, Narrative Accounts, and Commitment to a Volunteer Role. *Journal of Psychology 134* (4), 422-434.

Riggs, C. G. P. H. Muller. (2001). Employment and Utilization of Paraeducators in Inclusive Settings. *Journal of Special Education* 35(1): 54.

Rubin, Beth C. (2007). Learner Identity Amid Figured Worlds: Constructing (In)competence at an Urban High School. *The Urban Review,Vol.39.* No.2, 217-249.

Sarason, S. B. (1996). *Barometers of Change: Individual, Educational and Social Transformation.* San Francisco, Calif, Jossey-Bass, Incorporated Publishers.

Seidman, Irving (1998). *Interviewing as Qualitative Research.* New York and London, Teachers College Press.

Sfard, Anna and Prusak, Anna. (2005). Telling identities: In search of an analytic tool for investigating learning as a culturally shaped activity. *Educational Researcher, 34* (4), 14-22.

References

Shaywitz, Sally M. D. (2003). *Overcoming Dyslexia*. New York, Alfred Knopf.

Smith, S. D. (2000). From Paraprofessional to Credentialed Teacher: Motivational Factors That Influence Career Pathways in Special Education. *Unpublished doctoral dissertation,* University of San Francisco: 116.

SPeNSE, U.S. Office of Special Education Programs. (2000). *Fact Sheet: Study of Personnel Needs in Special Education.* Retrieved on November 15, 2002 in www.spense.org.

State of New Jersey. (2001). *Parental Rights in Special Education.* Department of Education, Trenton, NJ.

State of New Jersey. (2006). *New Jersey Administrative Code, Title 6A, Chapter 14, Special Education.* Revision adopted August 2, 2006. Effective September 5, 2006.

State of New Jersey. (2009). *District Factor Groups.* Retrieved on September 6, 2009 in http://www.state.nj.us/education/finance/sf/dfg.shtml.

State of New Jersey. (2009). *Historical Report Card.* Retrieved on September 6, 2009 in http://education.state.nj.us/rc/rc08/menu/21-5715.html.

Stryker, S. and Statham, A. (1985). Symbolic interaction and role theory. In G. Lindzey and E. Aronson (Eds.), *Handbook of social psychology* (Vol I, 3rd ed., pp. 311-378). New York: Random House.

Sullivan, Kathleen O'Connell (1998). Meeting the Challenge of Paraprofessional Training: An Application of the Competence Model. (Doctoral dissertation, Widener University. *Dissertation Abstract International, 59*, 889.

Tyack, David. (1976). "Ways of seeing: An essay on the history of compulsory school." *Harvard Education Review*, 46 (3), 355-389.

Tyack, David and Berkowitz M. (1977). "The Man Nobody Liked: Towards a Social History of the Truant Officer, 1840-1940." *American Quarterly Review* 29 1, pp 31-54

Tyack, David. and Cuban, Larry (1995). *Tinkering Toward Utopia: A Century of Public School Reform.* Cambridge, Massachusetts, Harvard University Press.

U.S. Census Bureau, (March 2005). College Degree Neary Doubles Annual Earnings, Census Bureau Reports. *U.S. Census Bureau News.* Retrieved on April 8,2007 from http://www.census.gov/PRess-Release/www/releases/archives/ education/004214.html

US Department of Education, Blue Ribbon School application (2006). Retrieved on April 22,2007 from http://www.ed.gov/programs/nclbbrs/2006/applications/ nj09_.pdf

U.S. Department of Education, as quoted in Staff Briefing: School Paraprofessional, Legislative Review and Programs

References

Committee (September 2006), Connecticut General Assembly.Retrieved on February 18, 2006 from http://www.cga.ct.gov/2006/pridata/Studies/PDF/School_P araeducators_%20Briefing_Report.PDF.

Water Wheel School (pseudonym) (2004). *Student Class Schedules*. Fieldtown, New Jersey: East Brighton-Fieldtown School District.

Watkins, Susan, and others. (1994). The Effectiveness of an Intervener Model of Services for Young Deaf-Blind Children. *American Annals of the Deaf, 139* (4) 404-409.

Wenger, Etienne. (1999). *Communities of Practice.* Cambridge University Press, Cambridge, England.

Werts, Margaret. Child Academic Engagement Related to Proximity of Paraprofessional. (1999) Doctoral dissertation, University of Pittsburgh, 1999. *Dissertation Abstract International, 59*, 3407.

Wolcott, Harry F. (2001). *Writing Up Qualitative Research,2nd ed.* Thousand Oaks, CA: Sage.

York-Barr, J. & Ghere, G. (2003). *Employing, Developing, and Directing Special Education Paraprofessionals in Inclusive Education Programs: Findings from a Multi-Site Case Study.* Minneapolis, Minn., University of Minnesota: 97.

Young, B., Simpson, R., Smith Myles, B., and Kamps, D.M. (1997). An examination in paraprofessional involvement in supporting students with autism. *Focus on Autism and Other Developmental Disabilities, 12*(1), 31-38, 48.

Index

Mary Hull is a learning consultant and school psychologist, working in a public school system in central New Jersey. She has taught in Florida, Georgia and Washington, D. C. as well.

At the time of this printing, she is completing her book *Conversations with Paraeducators* based upon *The Paraeducator: The Other Grown-Up In The Classroom*, with topics for paraeducators to consciously examine social behavior that engages students and forges partnerships between the adults in the classroom.

Dr. Hull is available to speak at conferences and conduct in-service training. She has recently presented in Pennsylvania at the National Convention for Paraprofessionals and in New Jersey for a school district in-service. She has been invited to speak in Connecticut, for the annual conference for the Paraprofessionals as Partners Initiative at the State Education Resource Center.

To contact her, visit her website at MaryWHull.org or email her at marywhull@gmail.com. She welcomes your input and feedback. She lives in Lawrenceville, New Jersey with her husband, Art.